Minnesota

by Joan Claire Graham and 36 Friends

The stories in *Minnesota Memories 5* are about real, not fictional people, places and events. Time may have sanded off a few rough edges, and repeating a story may have tempted the teller to embellish a detail or two, but these are all true stories told by Minnesota people.

As we grow older, we come to realize that our true stories have value. We use these stories to teach our young, to influence decisions, to affirm our humanity and to comfort and amuse one another. Despite the fact that our personal stories have tremendous historical, sociological and entertainment value, however, they will eventually have no value unless we write them down. Our own brain cells eventually give out, and audio and video tape tend to disintegrate over time. Stories that are merely passed down orally change and evolve with each telling--often beyond recognition. So, all things considered, paper and ink are the most dependable and archival media to which most people have easy access.

As I travel around the great state of Minnesota, looking for new *Minnesota Memories* stories and sharing those that have already been published, I encourage people to write just one extraordinary true story. Occasionally they follow my advice and send me the result.

You don't have to be from Minnesota to enjoy this book. People from around the world recognize kindred spirits in these tales. Told with humor and pathos, they not only ring true, but they capture the true essence of a place held dear by the tellers. These are not Ole and Lena jokes or hotdish parodies. These are real stories by and about real Minnesota people, places and events.

Joan Claire Graham
Purveyor of Memories

Contributors	Hometowns & Story Locales	Page
Joan Claire Graham	Albert Lea	5-27
Toni Babcock	South St. Paul, Minneapolis	29
Tom Bengtson	Minneapolis	39
Marilyn Mikulewicz Baranski	Winona, Rosemount, Apple Valley	34
Mary Jo Boots	Redwood Falls	82
Jeffrey L. Cardinal	Owatonna	90
Betty Jean Rueckert Collins	Minnesota Lake	175
Nick Cords	St. Clair	68
Lauretta Lynch Cords	St. Clair	65
Lloyd Deuel	Foreston, Milaca	73
Michael Finley	St. Paul	107
Marion Forderbrugen	Mankato	97
Graham S. Frear	Minnetonka Mills	111
Richard Hall	Austin	160
Judith Hambleton	Minnesota Lake	157
Donna Doyscher Hawkinson	Hollandale, Jackson	87
Betsy Hermanson	Mankato	46
Alyce Doyscher Jacobsen	Albert Lea, Waseca	28
Mary Kalkes James	Dundas	156
Bill King	Albert Lea	173
Neil Palmer Kittlesen	Frost	126
Kaye McMasters Klukow	Austin, Conger	147
Carol Keech Malzahn	Minnesota Lake	134
Don Matejcek	Owatonna	105
Kathy A. Megyeri	Owatonna, Northern Minnesota	56
Ken Nelson	Albert Lea, Hayward, Brainerd	115
Jesse Reisdorph	Morgan	149
Arvin Rolfs	Kenneth, Luverne	121
Dorothy Schnackenburg	St. Clair	50
Edgar Simmons	Bloomington	85
Stella Hanson Sorbo	Two Harbors, Alden	53
Alice Steilow	Clinton	141
Steve Swanson	Northfield	130
Anne Jenson Troska	Clarks Grove, Alden	151
Anastasia "Stacy" Vellas	Swatara	179
Arthur Vogt	Kellogg	55
Marian Porter Westrum	Albert Lea, Clarks Grove	170

ISBN: 0971-197-148

Minnesota Memories 5

Table of Contents

Lollipops and Underpants
by Joan Claire Graham

My dad, who did all the grocery shopping, took me with him one autumn day in 1949 when he went to Piggly Wiggly. I could hardly believe my good fortune when, in addition to all the canned corn and boxes of macaroni, he purchased a box of colorful and delicious-looking lollipops. This was stacking up to be a great day. Earlier my mom, who did all the other shopping, had held up two small pairs of underpants at Montgomery Wards and asked me which I liked best--the pink or the blue ones. Getting a new pair of underpants and a box of suckers on the same day was exciting and unprecedented.

My joy turned to despair, however, when I learned that I would not be allowed to keep either the lollipops or the underpants. Carol Adair, my new friend who lived four houses south, was celebrating her fourth birthday the next day, and I had been invited to her birthday party. Mother wrapped the lollipops and underpants in white tissue, tied a ribbon around the package, and told me I had to give the lollipops and underpants to Carol--to keep. This was my first birthday party, and I didn't know the protocol. What a bummer! My nose was completely out of joint.

The next day, party day, things got even worse. I got into a big fight with Mother. She wanted me to wear a brown dress that somebody's kid had handed down to me, and I didn't like it. I struggled and squirmed, cried, pouted and protested that I hated the brown dress and didn't want to go to the party anyway, but Mom won the fight by giving me a swat on the behind.

Wearing my brown dress and a lower lip that stuck out a mile, I stood grumpily on the back steps holding the gift with its bow facing downward and squinted into the warm October afternoon sun as Mom snapped a picture of her baby girl heading off to her first birthday party.

One hundred yards south, Adairs cheered me up somewhat with cake and games of "pin the tail on the donkey" and "duck, duck gray duck." An hour after I left my house in a state of despair, Florence Adair snapped another picture.

I looked somewhat less despondent with my mouth stretched into a manufactured smile, but I still felt uncomfortable in that awful brown dress. Carol, the owner of new underpants and a box of lollipops, looked radiant.

A month after Carol's birthday, in late November, I decided to host my own birthday party. I went around the neighborhood and invited Carol and her brother Denny, Bobby and Shorty--the two boys who lived at the north end of the block, and the little girl who lived behind us. Mother planned to celebrate my birthday with relatives in Mankato on Thanksgiving, and I neglected to tell her about the change of plans. As we ate breakfast that bleak Monday, the phone rang. Bobby and Shorty's mother called, and she wanted Mom to know that one of her boys would be late for my birthday party because he had a dentist appointment. "Birthday party?" my mom replied, "I didn't know we were having one. What time does it start?"

Mom immediately started flying around the house with her vacuum cleaner because she didn't want anybody to think she was a lousy housekeeper. Once the house was clean, she began to scramble through her pantry looking for birthday party food. She found a cake mix and some Hershey's syrup, so she made a cake and let partygoers pour syrup over it. It wasn't something any of us had ever tried before, but it was a big hit. I got to wear my red corduroy jumper--the one I liked. We played games like "button button, who's got the button?" and Bobby and Shorty gave me a nice little set of tin doll dishes with Mickey Mouse painted on them. Carol gave me some paper dolls, Denny gave me a box of crayons, and when all the kids had finally gone home, I felt fairly well compensated for my loss of those lollipops and underpants.

Florence and Mom--Finding a Place for Dennis
by Joan Claire Graham

Florence Adair was not surprised but she was disappointed to read a note on the back of her son Dennis' final kindergarten report card. The note said that he would not be able to move into first grade because there was no place for him in Albert Lea's public schools. Dennis had Down Syndrome, and although Albert Lea provided special education in 1950, they did not accept children like Dennis. Florence believed that this was wrong, so with no training as a leader, no formal education beyond secretarial school, and no previous experience in fighting for causes, she set out to change the educational system to include a place for Dennis.

Since the 1930s, Albert Lea's public schools had provided special education for children who were considered educable. Determination of educability was based on IQ tests and an assessment of the child's speech, physical independence, general health, and the probability that he or she might learn to read, write, and eventually become employable. If a child's measurable IQ fell below 50, or if he could not walk, speak clearly or hear, those in charge labeled him severely retarded or uneducable. These children were either institutionalized at the state school in Faribault or they stayed home. Although their formal education had been judged hopeless, their parents noticed that they were able to learn some things very well, so Florence stepped forward to speak on their behalf.

On September 3, 1950, Florence Adair took her case to the Kiwanis Underprivileged Children's Committee. The Albert Lea Tribune printed her plea to the community.

"Our child is a United States citizen. He is a resident of the city of Albert Lea, and yet outside of our own family circle, kind friends and neighbors, he is not accepted. Rather, he is neglected, ignored, or forgotten completely. There is no place in the public school system for him. The pity of it is, there truly is no place!

"But why shouldn't there be a place for him and the many other children like him, right here in Albert Lea? In a democracy such as ours, he should have equal rights with other children. He is just like any other child--he laughs and plays, loves affection and reacts to abuse the same as other children. True, he cannot compete with normal children in learning reading, writing and arithmetic, and he shouldn't be expected to.

"What can he learn? He can learn right from wrong, good conduct from bad conduct, how to take his place in the world, how to do things with his hands that will be useful to himself and to society--in other words, how to direct his energies to worthwhile things rather than to have no direction. We don't ask for the impossible for our child and the others like him. All we want is for him to be accepted for what he is. How can he learn? Just like any other child but in slow motion. Not only himself, but the community, will benefit from his being taught."

Florence then wrote a series of articles for the Albert Lea Tribune, and in the next six weeks at least a dozen stories informing the public about the need to provide opportunities for the retarded were published. Under the sponsorship of the Kiwanis, she helped organize the Parents and Friends of the Mentally Retarded, and within five months nine previously uneducable children were attending the Alpha Class each morning in the children's room of the public library. By spring her efforts expanded to encourage the city to sponsor a summer recreation program for special needs children and to help raise money for the continuation of the privately funded Alpha Class during the next school year.

Kiwanis members sold kids' day buttons, private pilots raised $600 by charging passengers a penny a pound for an aerial view of the city from their Piper Cubs, and miscellaneous donors came up with an additional $282. For a program that had been non-existent a year earlier, the progress of the Alpha Class was unbelievable, but the program hit a snag that fall when the teacher moved out of town.

After exhausting other possibilities, Florence walked a hundred yards over to our house and asked my mother, Cookie Graham, if she would take the job for $50 a month. Mom had an Associate of Arts degree in music and speech from McPhail and some teaching experience at Good Counsel Academy in Mankato during the Depression. Her own kids were in school so she agreed to take the 3-hour a day job--just until they found someone permanent. This temporary arrangement lasted 19 years.

Mom's initial work load involved visiting homebound kids with muscular dystrophy or other conditions on Mondays, teaching the regular class on Tuesdays, Wednesdays, and Thursdays, and providing an activity group for adults on Fridays. Florence Adair continued to appeal to city and state officials for improved programs, and parents and educators from Mankato, Austin, Owatonna and other towns started visiting Albert Lea to observe classes because outside St. Paul and Duluth, there were no programs for severely retarded children in Minnesota.

Energized by her progress but not satisfied to merely crusade locally, Florence led a delegation of parents to the legislature and won state funding for a public school program in Albert Lea for children like Dennis. In 1952 the state appropriated $410 for education and transportation to each qualified child. The hitch was that the class had to be taught by a fully certified special education teacher with at least two years of experience. With few job opportunities in the state and only the University of Minnesota offering the necessary training, qualified teachers were not lining the streets of Albert Lea, but eventually one showed up.

As original class members graduated into newly established public school programs and an adult activity center, the Alpha Class evolved into a private special education preschool. As community awareness and support grew, the class received the use of two west side rooms in the basement of the old courthouse, which had previously been used to store old Red Cross wicker wheelchairs.

To get into those rooms from the courthouse east side parking lot, attendees had to take two steps down, clomp through the dark boiler room, and take two steps up to the basement hallway. This little obstacle course was considered handicapped accessible, and grateful parents pitched in to transform those dingy rooms into a delightfully cheerful space with two child-size bathrooms.

The original parents' group morphed into the Freeborn County Association for Retarded Citizens and hooked up with other ARC chapters throughout the country. My mother and Florence Adair remained local leaders, and they were often called upon to write newsletter articles, speak at meetings, go before the legislature, attend conventions and do radio and television interviews.

Florence Adair remained a special education kingpin in Albert Lea, and The Alpha Class, with my mother as its teacher, moved to the more easily accessible Hammer School on Bridge and then to St. Theodore's on Clark Street. As years passed, public school services continued to expand and improve. Albert Lea Parks Department, under the direction of LeRoy Maas, established a summer recreational program, and as the town established new opportunities for retarded children and adults, more and more representatives from communities across the state visited Albert Lea to learn from the leaders. Educators from other towns would probably have figured out programs on their own eventually, but Florence and my mom strongly influenced the establishment and proliferation of special education during the 1950s and '60s.

Maintaining their private status, the Alpha Class received United Way funding and raised additional money by selling Christmas cards and gifts. The selling season started in July, when Mom visited a Minneapolis distributor to select merchandise samples. She would catalog items, organize an ordering system, and enlist the participation of parents and friends to host parties to sell holiday cards, wrapping paper, and gifts. The shipment of those orders would fill our front porch in late fall, and hostesses would pick up their loot to distribute to their partygoers. Eventually this fundraiser got so big that the shipment had to be delivered to the classrooms, where volunteers sorted and organized items in piles lined up on tables and the floor.

After hostesses had finally picked up all that merchandise, Mom had to collect all their checks, pay the distributor, and balance the books. The logistics of organizing and getting everything to come out right were overwhelming, so Mom called on her friend Florence to help with the accounting. Together they put in hundreds of fundraising hours, and each year the holiday card and gift fundraiser became more profitable.

Minnesota special education programs eventually won the support of Senator Hubert Humphrey, whose granddaughter had Down Syndrome, and in time, state and federal legislation mandated full access to free public education for all handicapped children from preschool through high school. Along with those laws came the requirement that all special education teachers be fully certified.

Although she had taken special education classes during summers, Mom did not qualify for Minnesota teacher certification. At the end of 1971, Mom stepped down as Alpha Class teacher, and The Freeborn County Association for Retarded Citizens held a banquet to honor her 19 years of service. She was not able to attend, however, because she was in the final stages of her unsuccessful battle with cancer.

The morning she died, I walked four houses south to tell Florence Adair, and we cried as we reminisced about the progress the two women had made in the field of special education. Florence's little boy Dennis, whose exclusion from Albert Lea's public schools had triggered her crusade to provide education for every child, was by then an adult, attending Albert Lea's very successful Daytime Activity Center and enjoying a full life that included working, swimming, bowling, and participating in a bell choir. His progress through Albert Lea's various programs for the retarded typified that of his many peers and classmates.

A few years later Florence was afflicted with Alzheimer's disease, and those of us who knew her in her glory days, her family, and members of her community, lamented the loss of her seemingly indomitable spirit. She died almost 40 years after she began her crusade to provide education for her son, and after living in an assisted care facility for several years, Dennis died in 2002.

There were other parents and friends who gave their time and talents to lay down the track for special education in Albert Lea and throughout the state of Minnesota. I cannot write about their work because I did not experience it first hand.

What I witnessed was the work accomplished by Florence and Mom, and after reflecting on their accomplishments for several decades, I feel proud to record their little piece of Minnesota history. Compelled by personal need and a sense of injustice, Florence unilaterally made the appeals that started the ball rolling, and she enlisted my mother as a loyal friend, dedicated teacher, and ally. They tackled a job that needed to be done, spent thousands of hours trying to make it work, and did a terrific job of paving the way for continued progress in the field of special education.

   The quality of life in Albert Lea and other places improved when Florence and Mom put their talents and determination to the test. Children who previously had been offered no place in school found their place, learned, matured, and thrived when given the chance. The story of this extraordinarily successful crusade led by two ordinary women, Florence Adair and Cookie Graham, deserves a spot alongside other significant achievements in Minnesota history books.

Left: Florence Adair, Minnesota's premiere special education crusader in the early '50s, celebrates her Silver Anniversary in the mid '60s with her son Dennis and her husband Floyd "Shorty." Photo courtesy of her daughter, Carol Adair Brune.

Right: Aquinata "Cookie" Graham, my mom. She was the Alpha Class teacher, special education advocate, and fundraiser chairman from 1952-1971. Photo by Love Cruikshank, Albert Lea Tribune.

Danger Lurks at the DMV
by Joan Claire Graham

I've always dreaded the prospect of doing business at any branch of the Department of Motor Vehicles, so when I moved back from Maryland, I put off getting my Minnesota driver's license, title transfer and tags as long as possible. Minnesota law allows new residents 60 days to register and take the test for a license, but it was impossible to meet that requirement. Since the Albert Lea office is only open on Thursdays and Fridays, I used that as an excuse. Halloween, Thanksgiving, my birthday, Christmas and New Years all landed on Thursdays or Fridays, so that kept me away from the courthouse all fall. When I finally took a hard look at my 2004 calendar, it occurred to me that I had run out of holidays and excuses. It was time to face the music and go down to the DMV.

As April Fool's Day approached, I found my Minnesota driver's manual and started cramming for the dreaded written test. Those things are always murder for me because I have a tendency to think too much. For example, if the test question states, "If you drink you should not drive," the answer they want everybody to mark is "True." You should not drink and drive.

I have a tendency to read such a question, however, and think, "Drink what? Water? Coffee? Orange Crush? Surely they must not expect people to drive dehydrated. They might get sick. That would be risky. This must be a trick question. I'll just mark 'False.'" I then feel a rush of shame as the examiner shakes her head while making red checks all over my answer sheet. Like I said, I don't do well on those tests.

But this time I studied my Minnesota driver's manual and resolved to engage in no critical thinking during the exam. I noticed that state law now requires licensees to bring along a birth certificate and any change of name verification such as a marriage license, Social Security card, or divorce decree.

What luck, I thought. I was born right here in Albert Lea, and my name is now the same as on my birth certificate, my Maryland license and the only Social Security card I've ever owned. I got that Social Security card laminated when I was a kid, so it has held up well through 50 years.

I steeled myself for taking my test, standing in lines and dealing with bureaucrats, gathered my credentials, and headed for the Albert Lea DMV shortly after noon on a crisp April Friday.

This particular episode of my life started so great that my optimism soared as I imagined that I might just sail through it without a hitch. I entered the exam room on the second floor of the courthouse and picked up a test booklet from a woman behind a desk. After clearing my head, I surprised myself by checking off all the correct answers. After I passed my vision test and handed my credentials to a harmless-looking woman on the ground floor, my progress came to a screeching halt.

"You did not spell your name correctly," she said. I assured her that I have been spelling my name correctly for as long as I can remember. "No," she said. "On your birth certificate, your middle name is spelled "C-l-a-r-e." I assured her that my birth certificate is wrong. I spell my middle name with an "i" in the middle--always have--C-l-a-i-r-e. I believe the other spelling--with no i-- is the preferred spelling for males.

I produced my Maryland license, my automobile title, and my Social Security card to prove that my middle name has an "i" in it. The clerk said that my Social Security card was not an acceptable form of identification because it is laminated. Never mind that I laminated it before lamination became illegal. Never mind that I have saved the Social Security administration a few dollars in clerical fees and postage by conscientiously hanging on to my original card for five decades. That card was worthless at the Albert Lea DMV. The clerk said that my Maryland auto title was not acceptable identification either because the information on it was based on the erroneous information on my Maryland license and on my laminated Social Security card.

I assured her that if she wanted me to, I could go home and get further proof--a baptismal certificate, school report cards, high school and college diplomas, marriage certificate, passport, my parents' will, my mortgage, my Minnesota Lifetime Teaching Certificate, numerous by-lines and the program from the 1952 LeRand Studio tap dancing recital. What more proof would a clerk at the Albert Lea courthouse need to verify the correct spelling of my middle name?

"It doesn't matter what those things say," she replied. I will not be able to issue you a Minnesota driver's license unless you sign an affidavit stating that all those other documents are wrong. Your name on those documents does not match the name on your birth certificate."

I asked to speak to her supervisor, and she spent quite a bit of time on the phone trying to find and summon that supervisor. Business at the Albert Lea DMV came to a standstill as all available personnel focused on my case, and the line behind me extended out the door and all the way down the hallway.

When the supervisor arrived, I explained once again that I had been spelling my middle name with an "i" ever since I knew how to write. Before that, other people spelled it that way for me. She shook her head and said that she was sorry. "You're either going to have to sign the affidavit stating that you've been spelling your name wrong, or you won't get your license."

"Well, I think whoever wrote my name on that birth certificate back in 1945 got it wrong. I want to sign an affidavit to that effect and keep my "i." I don't want to mess up all my other documents by signing this affidavit that in effect says all my other documents are wrong. Besides, I like having that extra vowel. Whenever I play that party game where we try to see how many words we can make from the letters of our names, it always gives me a competitive edge to have that "i."

She was not amused. "Your original identification document is your birth certificate. That is what we must go by. If you really believed there was something wrong with your birth certificate, you would have corrected it before now."

"I can assure you," I replied, "that if any individual or government agency had ever questioned the absence of my birth certificate "i" when I applied for my passport, driver's license, marriage license or Social Security card, I would have tended to the matter and corrected the error that most certainly exists on my birth certificate. Before today, nobody ever noticed or cared."

The woman of steel shook her head and looked serious as she delivered the fatal blow. "You can sign the affidavit now, and we'll give you your license and title with your middle name spelled C-l-a-r-e. Ever since 9-11, we've been instructed to red flag all discrepancies and correct them."

Well, now it made sense. It's all about 9-11. Since so many Al Qaida members and other terrorists have fit the profile of hometown middle-aged guilt-ridden Catholic women who specialize in writing memoir and giving feel-good speeches to service organizations and residents of retirement centers, we must all do what we can to preserve the American Way of Life by ensuring that this particular would-be suicide bomber spells her middle name without an "i." As the absurdity of my situation sank in, I noticed the line behind me was getting longer and more agitated.

I weighed my options. It was almost 3 p.m. After investing more than two hours in this endeavor, I was only a signature away from getting my Minnesota driver's license, plates and title transfer. Signing the affidavit would be giving in to coercion, but since it was Friday, my next opportunity to come down here and go head to head with Barney Fife and Albert Lea's DMV terrorist-buster squad would be next Thursday. I knew I could prove my point and retain my "i," but I didn't know that I would have the determination or inclination to come back in six days and resume this conflict. So although it was the cowardly and wrong thing to do, I signed the affidavit, and the collective sigh of relief from dozens of Freeborn County citizens standing in line behind me blew me right out the front door of the courthouse.

I've always dreaded the prospect of doing business with all those DMVs in the many places where I've lived--the lines, the confusion, the long waits, the hassles, the tests. But my Albert Lea experience introduced a new dreaded element--danger. Let this be a warning to all: Be careful at the Albert Lea DMV. Those guys down there are dangerous. They can wear you down; they can force you to sign an affidavit; they can even put your "i" out.

Laughing All the Way
by Joan Claire Graham

Two public schools sat within two blocks of my childhood home, but since my family belonged to Albert Lea's minority group, the Catholics, I had to march right past one of those schools on my way to St. Theodore's. It was only about a half mile farther, but to a kid, that was a lot of steps.

For a few years, the city bus ran right past my house, and Mom let me ride it in the morning if the weather was cold. After driving all over town, the bus would drop me off two blocks short of St. Theodore's and fifteen minutes late for mass. I usually walked, but I didn't walk alone.

Not many Catholics lived on the west side of town, but Carol Bergen did. She lived at least six blocks beyond where I lived, so when she walked to St. Theodore's, Carol had to walk past two public schools. I am sure God was pleased with her effort.

Our walks to school were the best part of my entire nine years of parochial education because we had so many good laughs along the way. Carol stopped at my house around 7:45, and as we started walking together, we told each other about our dreams, which usually got us laughing because they were so ridiculous. Next we went into a discussion of last night's television shows: *I Love Lucy, Candid Camera, Red Skelton* and *The Ed Sullivan Show.* We'd repeat situations and punch lines and laugh as if they were new. We'd stop at the bakery downtown to buy a fresh raised donut or a caramel roll for breakfast. We couldn't eat before communion, but the nuns would let us eat at our desks at the beginning of the school day, and, because we were so religious and interested in attending mass and receiving communion every day, our moms let us have a few cents to spend at the bakery.

Mass attendance was optional, but it showed up as a report card grade under the subject title "growth in religious habits." I needed all the good marks I could get, so I tried to arrive on time for 8 o'clock mass as often as I could. I skipped breakfast so I could receive Holy Communion, thus insuring at least one "A" on my report card and fresh bakery treats almost every day, a winning combination.

Once we got to church, everything made us crack up, and sometimes we would stifle our laughter so much we thought we'd burst. Monsignor Mangen had hay fever, and often, in the middle of mass, he would start sneezing with the sound, "har-umph." Sometimes there would be 20 or 30 "har-umphs" in a row--all in perfect cadence. He was probably miserable, but his endless "har-umphage" made us laugh, and sometimes a nun would notice our shaking shoulders and tap one of us and tell us to behave. This caused more laughter!

On one trip to school we discussed a pickpocket we'd seen on a variety show. We couldn't figure out how he did it, but he went through the audience and took wallets and jewelry off people who were shocked to discover he had their stuff. He stole one guy's wallet three times! We were still having fun discussing how amazing this guy was when we had to quiet down and go into church. Just as we were opening the door, something shiny caught my eye. I looked down and saw Carol's watch drop off her wrist because the band had come unfastened. She didn't feel it or notice it fall, so I scooped it up and put it in my right pocket.

When we got to our places in church, she sat on my left. As everything got quiet except for Monsignor Mangen's sneezing, out of the corner of my eye I caught sight of Carol swiping a handkerchief that had been peeking out of my left pocket. A few minutes later she nudged me and handed me my handkerchief--an obvious homage to last night's television pickpocket. I smiled, took my handkerchief, and handed her the watch that had fallen. What a hilarious joke! She was highly amused, and couldn't figure out how I got her watch off her left wrist. Of course, we got into trouble for laughing like maniacs. Everything that might be mildly funny anywhere else is hilariously funny if it happens in church, when you're not supposed to laugh.

As my baby boomer generation expanded, St. Theodore's accommodated just the younger kids because even the Catholics needed two schools. Kids in the upper grades crowded onto a single school bus that made several trips after morning mass to take us out to our brand new St. Mary's school on the north side of town. If the weather was nice, we offered to walk the additional mile to the other school to save the bus driver from having to make so many shuttles and to give ourselves some additional free time to find more things to laugh about.

It didn't take much to get us laughing. One time we tied ourselves in knots because a woman we knew kept referring to her tulips as "early bloomers." The word "bloomers" sent us over the top. We laughed at funny sounding Latin words in songs we sang in church, and we nearly died laughing when a boy in school read a math problem and said, "Four leebs and six oozes minus three leebs and two oozes...." He didn't know about the abbreviations for pounds and ounces, and we got endless laughter mileage out of that one. On the playground a girl caught a muddy kick ball right smack in her face, and for weeks--even years afterward, we laughed whenever we talked about her surprise, indignation, and the way she looked with her face full of mud.

We both played clarinets in band, so we got out of class together for our weekly lesson with our director, Cec Turner. He was a card, and a protestant, and we laughed when he told us about the time he got in trouble for playing "Away in a Manger," written by Martin Luther. Sister Sean, the principal, ran into the band room and halted the performance declaring indignantly, "We don't play that song here, Mr. Turner!" He imitated her when he told the story, and we laughed every time we retold it.

One time Cec decided he'd teach his little band how to march. He lined us up in six or eight columns in the school gym and had us march to the end, pivot and march back between the oncoming columns while playing our simplest march. We discovered the challenge of learning to play while marching as our instruments bounced around and sour notes and shaky tones warbled out. Unaccustomed to our band sounding like a warped record while we smashed into each other on the turn-arounds, Carol and I convulsed with laughter, and we laughed all the way home.

We volunteered to dust the school on Friday afternoons. With feather dusters in hand, we'd make a few passes over the statue of Mary that stood by the front door and then head in to the kitchen to see if there was any leftover cheese, celery sticks or Jell-O to swipe from the fridge. The cooks made red finger Jell-O in a big pan and cut it in squares. One time the principal caught us in the kitchen just as we had each put a whole chunk of the stuff in our mouths. She said, "What are you doing, girls, having lunch?" I swallowed it in one gulp and managed, "No sister," and Carol had tears running down her cheeks--either from Jell-O stuck in her throat or from trying not to laugh. We had new material for our walk home.

On the way home, well out of earshot of anyone who would be offended, Carol would start chanting, "har-umph, har-umph, har-umph, har-umph," and I would start singing, "The Campbells are coming, tra-la, tra-la" and then launch into a chorus of "The Irish Washerwoman" with Carol's sneeze sounds as my back-up band. Performing this act for puzzled passers-by always made us laugh like crazy. We'd throw our heads back and laugh full throttle. Mother used to say that she could hear us coming home before she could see us. While walking home past the high school one day I felt something wet drop on my head. Thinking it was a high school kid with a squirt gun in the second story band room, I looked up and yelled something like, "Hey, you guys up there, knock it off." When I reached up to my wet head, however, I had a hand full of bird doo. Carol and I laughed with wild abandon.

We made up a song about Father Engels, the young priest who taught at our school, and walked along the sidewalk singing it to the tune of "Wringle-Wrangle," and we laughed uproariously. We wrote a parody of the tearjerker ballad, "Teen Angel." Our version went, "That fateful night the car was stalled upon the railroad tracks--I pulled you out by the leg and used you for a jack." Over and over, we'd sing and laugh.

Our walks ended when our class of about 25 kids graduated from Catholic school in 1961. We moved on to public high school, where we blended into a class of 400, found new friends, and drifted apart.

My laughing pal, Carol Bergen

I attended Catholic school for nine years. That's about 1600 school days or 3200 walking trips to school and back--thousands of miles-- and I walked the majority of those miles with Carol Bergen. I've had many other friends since the days when Carol was my pal, but I have never had a friend with whom I laughed every single day, year after year, mile after mile. Maybe it was our age or the fact that strict Catholic school rules made us especially prone to laugh as a release. Maybe we were the comedy team of the century, or maybe we just cracked each other up. Whatever it was, it sure was fun.

Rite of Passage
by Joan Claire Graham

Transition from childhood to adolescence was marked by acquiring certain grown-up privileges in the '50s. Boys got BB guns and air rifles, but as girls edged into double digit ages, we began obsessing about three tangible, socially visible accouterments we believed we needed to prove to the world that we weren't exactly children anymore: We wanted nylons, lipstick and high heels. Our mothers talked to other mothers to come up with a consensus about when they might permit us to use these symbols of maturity without enduring negative judgment from church or community members, and they strictly enforced their decision. The months and years we were forced to wait seemed endless.

Of course we couldn't dress up and wear lipstick to school, but church was considered a safe and reasonable place where we would be allowed to debut our symbols of female maturity. The year we were 13 years old, everybody's mother decided pale lipstick, seamless nylons, and high heels would be acceptable to wear with our Easter dresses--provided they were those squatty looking heels that were only an inch and a half high. When I went to buy mine, they didn't have any my size so I ended up with two-inch heels--which put me in a category by myself because they actually looked like pumps.

You couldn't wear pumps with bare legs, so Mom let me buy nylons at J.C. Penney's. Penney's advertised a special deal from time to time--two pairs for a dollar. Stock was kept in flat boxes filed neatly behind a store counter, and a clerk wearing white gloves would count out how many pairs a customer wanted and wrap them in tissue arranged in a flat folder. Once the nylon stockings were purchased, I faced a question of how to hold them up. I didn't have a garter belt, so Mom gave me a soft, puckered cotton panty girdle that had amazing stretch qualities. At rest it could fit a baby--stretched out it could fit a truck.

Easter Sunday arrived. I hitched up my suntan colored seamless nylons to the garter fasteners on my panty girdle, slipped into my new pink linen, rolled collar, empire-waist Easter dress that I had found at Wallaces a few days earlier, carefully applied my Max Factor natural lipstick that looked orange in the tube yet turned pale pink on the lips, stepped into my high heels, and finished off my ensemble with a new spring hat and gloves. For a moment in front of my bedroom mirror, I believed I looked as beautiful as the girls in *Teen* magazine, but my confidence was short lived.

My brother, a high school senior, laughed maniacally as I wobbled down the steps to meet the family in the living room, and my mother's somewhat tepid defense was, "I think she looks just fine." Feeling that peer judgment was usually closer to my own assessment of modern situations, I began to lose faith that I could carry off this Easter parade charade. My dad, however, always the first one out of the gate, was already in the car, honking its horn. There was no time to turn back. My coming out party was imminent.

As usual, my dad parked a block down Clark Street, with his car facing homeward. He was a rigid practitioner of the fast getaway after mass, so we had to pay the price. I soon learned there was a vast difference between walking around my small bedroom in high heels and striding a hundred yards down a city sidewalk.

As I walked along, trying to keep my ankles straight and my countenance cheery, I began to take on a new fear. What if those fasteners let go and my nylons fell down? Without any previous experience with garters, I didn't know how dependable they were. I imagined them letting go like a sling shot--shooting me in the rear with their metal hardware and rubber knob and forcing me into shame by dropping my hose to my ankles. As I began to believe this was a real possibility, I started taking shorter steps--thinking that if I felt the garter give way I could somehow save face by grabbing my falling-down nylons between my knees.

We greeted a few friends outside, then settled down in our usual pew at the back of the church. Mass began, and each time I had to stand up, kneel down or sit, I prayed--really prayed-- that my garters would hold. The fact that they hadn't let go yet only prolonged the tension and my belief that they were eventually going to snap.

When it came time to walk up to the communion rail, I felt trapped. Choosing to sit out communion on Easter Sunday was not an option; I had to stand up with everyone else and go up there. In fact, I had to walk the whole length of the church up the center aisle, kneel at the communion rail, and return down the side aisle. My knees were shaking, and my ankles were wobbling as I minced along, and I had eaten off all my Max Factor lipstick with lip-biting worry. Believing all eyes were focused on me, I broke out in a sweat, and as I edged toward the communion rail, I could feel rivulets drizzling from my armpits to my sides. Could sweat eventually drip out of the bottom of my dress? Add another risk factor to this already terrifying experience.

As I rose from the communion rail to return down the side aisle to our pew at the back, I caught the smiling face of my friend's mother. She was probably just expressing an Easter greeting, or perhaps noticing another of her daughter's friends all dolled up for Easter, but I was sure she was laughing because she could see that my nylons were about to fall down, my ankles were wobbling, my lipstick was long gone and I was sweating like a butcher. I looked down and tried to appear normal as I minced back to join my family in the last row.

Thanks to Dad's immutable quick getaway routine, I managed to avoid after-mass socializing or comparing of outfits with my friends. When I got home I raced up to my room, kicked off my shoes, ditched my nylons, and wriggled out of the panty girdle. I touched up my lipstick, found some anklets and flats, and went downstairs, where I settled in to eat jelly beans from my Easter basket and read the Sunday funnies. I did not complete the transition from child to young woman that day. I still had a long way to go.

My Irreplaceable Costume Doll
by Joan Claire Graham

I was crazy about dolls when I was a kid, and I still remember most of my dolls that I received as Christmas and birthday gifts. I got a rubber baby doll named Agnes when I was 2. When I was 3, I got a plaster composition baby doll, and when I showed it to Uncle Al, he said it was handsome. I thought he said Hanson, so that's what I named it. I had a baby doll with sleepy eyes, a Raggedy Ann, tiny twins with matching outfits, a Topsy doll, a walking doll, and Tiny Tears. Mom dressed one doll like a cowgirl, and I named her Dale Evans. All my dolls had names, and I loved to play with them and dress them in the clothes Mom made.

When I was 8 years old in 1953, Mom gave me the most wonderful doll I've ever seen. She bought an 18" girl doll at Woolworth's, and in the months before Christmas, after everyone else was asleep, she spent hours designing and making a beautiful doll wardrobe that included a bridal gown, pajamas and robe, ice and roller skating outfits, an Easter dress, a prom formal, a Mexican fiesta costume, a tap dancing costume, a drum majorette uniform, a ballet tutu, and a Miss America outfit with a pink satin gown, velvet-lined cape, and a sparkling crown. She called it a costume doll, and I loved it.

Mom paid incredible attention to every detail of every costume. Each skirt was lined and trimmed with lace, fur, applique, or sequins. Each skirt contained ample yardage to ensure a rich look, and each bodice contained darts to ensure a perfect fit. Each opening was faced and finished with snaps, hooks or buttons.

Mom made tiny panties and bras to match each outfit, along with slips and hats. At our very well-stocked Woolworth's store, she bought an assortment of shoes, socks, skates, boots, and slippers to go with every outfit. There was a little baton to go with the majorette dress. I don't know where she got the inspiration for each costume, but she designed everything using no patterns and sewed each piece by hand.

Mom worked on this project for several months. A night owl, she would take out her sewing after everybody else went to bed, and she would work late into the night. I had no idea the project was in the works, so the gift came as a complete surprise that Christmas. Casting aside my usual lack of organization, I kept this exquisite ensemble and the doll in perfect order in a trunk that had a dowel for hanging all the dresses and drawers for keeping all the accessories. I liked to place the doll in a stand and display it on my dresser-- changing the outfit every few days. My costume doll was my treasured toy and the envy of my friends.

For several years, Mom made the doll new costumes for special occasions. After I got too old to play with dolls, I put the doll in the trunk with all her beautiful costumes and hoped I'd someday have a little girl who would enjoy it as much as I had. Like most of my outgrown toys, the trunk went up to the attic.

When my mother died in 1972, I felt especially glad to have such a monument to her creativity and skill. It was the only toy I cared about keeping. Since I moved around a lot, however, I kept my costume doll in my dad's attic. When my first daughter was born in 1975, I knew she was destined to love that costume doll.

My dad remarried in 1975, and while he and his new wife were off on a honeymoon, they invited me to come to the house and take away whatever I wanted to keep. My very fussy baby was only a couple of weeks old, but I managed to drive to Albert Lea and go to the attic and gather a few boxes I wanted to take. I wrote my name on the trunk and a few other boxes and left a note for my dad saying I would come back and haul everything when I didn't have a car full of baby paraphernalia and when I had some help and was feeling a little less overwhelmed. Between having to travel and deal with a colicky baby, extreme heat in the attic and residual weakness from a C-section, I didn't feel I could carry two or three loads to the car, and there wasn't anybody who could help me. As an afterthought, I took the doll out of the trunk and brought it home with me.

A few months later I came back with the requisite strength, cargo space, and work crew. We pushed open the heavy attic door and went to the place where I had left my costume doll trunk.

To my astonishment, the trunk was gone. It wasn't as if anyone had been cleaning house. The other boxes I had labled were there. The attic was chock full of the usual stuff--old clothes, holiday ornaments, out of season clothes, an old mattress, cast-off furniture, old lamp shades, scrapbooks and suitcases. But my trunk, my wonderful trunk containing a doll wardrobe sewn and designed by my mother, was gone.

I searched every nook and cranny, but my treasure was gone. No, my dad didn't remember anything about it. Had he sold it at a garage sale? He didn't remember. Had he given it away? Had he seen my name written in big letters on a very familiar trunk? No, he didn't remember.

Thinking that someone in town might have bought it at a garage sale or received my trunk full of doll clothes as a gift from my dad, I wrote a letter to Love Cruikshank, a columnist for the Albert Lea Tribune. I described the trunk and its contents and asked if anyone had seen it. She published my letter, along with her plea to her readers to help me get the trunk back. I still had the doll, and all the clothes in the trunk were tailored to fit it. They wouldn't fit most dolls.

I wanted my trunk back, and I held out for a miracle because my mother sewed those clothes with her own hands, and they were the nicest gifts she ever gave me. If there ever was a place in my life for a miracle, this was it. But nothing came of my quest. Throughout the years I returned to the attic dozens of times, thinking it might magically reappear. Until we sold the house in 1993, I always expected to find my costume doll trunk in a tucked away spot that I had previously overlooked. No luck.

As years went by, I bought various dolls and doll wardrobes to compensate for my loss. In the '80s, I bought American Girl dolls for my two daughters, and they kept their collections organized nicely in trunks that I also bought from that company.

Those dolls are very nice, and they're somewhat similar to my costume doll. When Pleasant Rowlands started sending her American Girl Doll catalogs, she wrote a little story on the back that was supposed to explain why she started manufacturing and selling her dolls. It said, "In a forgotten corner of the basement of an old museum I found a doll trunk--a forgotten treasure of some long-ago child." I felt sure the story that inspired her American Girl collection was the story of my lost my doll trunk and the costumes it contained. Maybe it was.

Somebody somewhere has that trunk and all the costumes it contains. The costumes were too nice to throw away, and the trunk would never have been cast aside as an empty trunk because anyone who picked it up would have detected a full load inside it.   I still have the doll, although she needs to be re-strung because all the elastic that used to hold her arms and legs on gave out years ago. I should take her out and fix her, but I can't seem muster up whatever it takes to do it.   I still have the costume she wore when I took her--the Mexican fiesta outfit.

It has been 30 years since I saw those other lovely costumes my mom designed and sewed, and I still feel a profound sense of loss.   I know I should let it go, but I don't want to because the optimist in me continues to cling to hope. Every time I go to a second-hand store, garage sale or estate sale I keep a sharp lookout for that trunk or for any trace of even one of my doll costumes. An old piece of doll clothing or a 50-year old trunk wouldn't mean much to the person trying to sell it, but to me it would be a treasure.

My costume doll, before we put her in the trunk, Christmas 1953.

Joan Claire Graham is a retired teacher, freelance writer and editor who believes that her job as purveyor of Minnesota Memories is the best job ever. The mother of two incredible adult daughters and two geriatric cats, she enjoys traveling around Minnesota and speaking to groups.

A Wedding Day Story
by Alyce "Penny" Doyscher Jacobsen

The wedding was over and the reception too. The bride and groom were heading north out of Albert Lea on Highway 13 in their borrowed car. We had first night reservations at the Saulpaugh Hotel in Mankato, but we planned to spend the rest of our honeymoon week along Lake Superior's North Shore.

It was August 31, 1948, a perfect summer day, still warm and sunny at 5:30 as we drove through Waseca. We realized, "It's awfully early. How could it still be afternoon?"

Our wedding was at 3 p.m., and the reception followed in the First Presbyterian Church's Westminster Hall. By 4:45, I had thrown my bouquet, and there was nothing to do but leave.

We didn't own a car, and Jake had kept quiet about whose vehicle we were borrowing. Three possibilities were parked near the church's back door. The groomsmen didn't know which one to decorate so we successfully avoided the typical tin can-streamer-just-married pandemonium.

This was 1948, back in the days when many couples--even engaged couples--waited until after the wedding the sleep together, and we were waiting. However, driving through Waseca on our wedding day, we looked at each other and said, "It's too early to go to bed." So we stopped at a play park, and for fifteen minutes, Jake pushed me on a swing.

The park now houses a library building and the swings are long gone, but we still smile whenever we drive through Waseca.

Alyce grew up in Hollandale and worked as a speech and language clinician. She has two grown sons and lives with her husband in Albert Lea.

Silver Strands Wove a Golden Memory
by Toni Babcock

I stood beside the old dresser in Grandma's tiny bedroom, knowing I was about to witness something strange and wonderful. Grandma was pulling little metal hairpins out of her thick, sturdy braid, wrapped like a crown on the top of her head. Soon she would be transformed before my 5-year-old eyes. It was almost mystical, Grandma unwrapping and brushing her long, silver-gray, waist-length hair. I was transfixed.

When I think of that magical experience, it was as if all of Grandma's secret dreams and aspirations flowed through those beautiful strands of silver hair. When it was time, she would weave them back into a careful braid and wrap them safely around her head. I can't help but wonder about all of Grandma's dreams and wishes. Did she have dreams for us wrapped in those silver strands of hair? Did she reach her aspirations on that little farm in Minnesota? I know the myriad of family who sprang from her, tied to her as tightly as that carefully knit braid, will have her to thank in part for reaching theirs.

Grandma will always be remembered as a storyteller, artist and musician. I remember warm summer nights, climbing the yellow wooden steps to the upstairs bedroom, in anticipation of being cuddled and cajoled to sleep by her funny stories and silly knock-knock jokes.

Whenever she found time, Grandma would paint beautiful pictures on whatever usable surface was handy; backs of calendars, mirrors, wood or canvas (when she could get it), and even an old drum skin. She encouraged my talents too. Inspired by her artistry, I colored a family of swans with crayons when I was 9. Grandma was so proud, she framed it under a glass tray, which I still have.

She shared her love of music and her musical gifts with everyone she knew, even whistling bird songs native to the region, which we loved to hear. Grandma made the best of the life that she had, with what little she had, and I never heard her complain.

Life changes come with loss. Some years after Grandpa Klement passed away, Grandma knew it wouldn't be good to live alone. She decided to marry a man named Joe. She also decided it was time to cut her hair. That long, silver-gray, beautiful waist-length hair was becoming too hard for her to take care of; we all knew that, and life was changing for Grandma.

When she passed away a few years later, Grandma left such wonderful memories. I believe this was her gift to her daughters, and to their daughters. For it seems to me, in some magical, mysterious way, Grandma's secret dreams and aspirations were woven into ours.

Toni Babcock hails from South St. Paul with her husband Kerry. She enjoys memoir and travel writing and hopes to pass her love of the great outdoors to her seven grandchildren.

A Brains Over Brawn Canoe Rescue
by Toni Babcock

My husband Kerry and I decided, on a whim, to participate in a paddle and portage race on Lake Nokomis one summer in Minneapolis. We entered the mixed recreational category, which consisted of two laps around the lake and one lengthy portage.

On a perfect afternoon the week before the race, we headed out to the lake to check out the course. The lake water was not flat, nor was it too choppy. The air was just breezy enough to offer a little wind resistance and increase the challenge. Several sailboats dotted the lake, taking advantage of the prime weather.

We ran the course once, when Kerry noticed something odd in the middle of the lake. It was a canoe with nobody in it - at least that's what it looked like. The canoe was extremely low in the lake, almost submerged. We abruptly drew the boat right and paddled out to investigate. When we were about 150 yards away, we could see two heads bobbing in the water next to the boat. A sailboat that whisked by them couldn't seem to stop.

As we got closer to their canoe, I knew Kerry was mentally rehearsing a rescue technique he read about in *Path of the Paddle*, a guidebook for canoeists by Bill Mason. The technique is called "canoe over canoe" rescue. I had every reason to believe he could pull it off.

Kerry has an uncanny ability to keep a canoe afloat. I recall one instance when our boat was pinned broadside against a fallen tree anchored from a riverbank on Rice Creek - the classic "strainer." It was springtime, and the water was high and fast. As we tipped dangerously to the side, water just barely began to flow over the upstream gunwale. I was thinking, "Okay, this is interesting-- now we are about to get sucked under the current," when I heard Kerry shout, "Don't let it happen, Toni!" Somehow he managed to pop the boat back up, preventing it from being pulled under the fallen tree. Who knows what tangled web hid under the current? Kerry attributes his paddling ability to the simple fact that he doesn't like to get wet. Hey, whatever works! (I think we had an angel watching over us as well).

As we approached the flooded canoe on Lake Nokomis that summer day, we saw two boys around 13 years old, hanging onto one side of their boat. They looked exhausted and agitated, one boy snapping at the other to "quit letting more water into the boat!" It was obviously hopeless by then. The canoe couldn't have gotten much more water in it. One boy's life jacket was thrown loosely over his neck but the other had his secured. They were so absorbed in their predicament, they never saw us coming until we were practically on top of them.

"Hey, you guys!" Kerry called out. They stopped squabbling and looked up. "We can help you!" Hopeful, but a bit skeptical, they listened as Kerry assured them he could get them out of the water and back in their boat, no problem. "I read about it in a book."

Then my self-professing control freak husband got the situation under control and started giving instructions. There was no time to lose, and with an audience of a few sailboats whizzing nearby to investigate, we set ourselves to the task.

We positioned the boats directly side by side, and Kerry carefully pulled up on the gunwale of their canoe and rolled it over, upside down. "You boys get behind our boat, one on each side and stabilize it," Kerry instructed.

They slid along their boat and around to the stern of our canoe and held on. No panic - so far so good. We then arranged the canoes in a "T" configuration with our boat as the top of the T. My job was to stabilize the bow of our canoe, as the boys stabilized the stern, while Kerry pulled off the crucial maneuver.

I carefully leaned over the left side of the bow and "waddled" my paddle left and right like a beaver tail on the surface of the lake. This helped to keep us from rolling over as Kerry pulled up one end of their turned over canoe and hoisted it slowly up and onto the center of our boat crosswise. He then carefully rolled it right side up and pushed it across the center of our boat and back onto the lake on the opposite side. Voila! The boys were noticeably impressed. "Wow!" one of them exclaimed.

Getting them back into the boat was the easy part. With both canoes hugged side by side and held together by a firm grip, the boys mustered up enough strength to hoist themselves back into their boat - one at a time. Whew! Their floating paddles had been retrieved. Mission accomplished. Evidently a sharp turn had led them to this disaster. I suggested they kneel in their boat to lower their center of gravity, giving their canoe more stability. A few more friendly exchanges took place, and off they went, paddles in hand.

Later, as we strapped our canoe onto the top of our van, a black car flashed by with a boy hanging out the window waving and shouting, "Thank you!" We both stared blankly, thinking it was a sarcastic remark from someone thanking us for using up one and one-half parking spots by the beach with our bulky van. Then recognizing it was one of the boys, we smiled and waved back. In fact, I think we smiled all the way home.

The Glamour of Jackie
by Marilyn Mikulewicz Baranski

As many young women growing up in the 1960s, I was enthralled by the glamour of Jackie Kennedy. She was a role model for me when I was in those very impressionable teenage years.

I had come from a very functional world. Everyone I knew lived by a work ethic where things had a purpose and had been designed to be used. Just because something was pretty didn't count. The question was always, "What do you use it for?"

Functional is fine and necessary, but I read about Jackie's world and longed for the designer clothes, the class, the perfection, the confidence and the excitement and romance of the life she lead. Mind you, I never even came close, but I was totally inspired by tales of her finishing school, Vassar, Oleg Cassini designs, her French ancestry and just her style and trend setting ways as she influenced America and me. I had the little pillbox hat--well actually mine was a wig hat in the shape of a pillbox hat that you could comb whichever way you wanted. I don't think Cassini ever designed one for Jackie exactly like it.

Years went by, our beloved president was killed, but the world was still under the influence of the beautiful and mysterious Jackie. I was going to my college prom, and my desire for glamour again raised its weak little head. I bought a Cassini-like dress in a shade of soft yellow that I convinced myself was very Parisian. I found yellow shoes that peeked out as my little foot took a step.

Did I mention that my feet were smaller than Jackie's size 9 1/2? I probably inherited my grandmother's feet. My grandmother had fainted on the corner of Concord and something or other in the 1930s when she squeezed her size 6 feet into a size 4 shoe. But I digress.

The afternoon of my prom, I had my hair done in a little shop someplace on Fifth Street in Winona. My hair didn't exactly look like Jackie's, but hey, close enough!! On the way home I stopped at a drug store and bought a set of artificial nails. I thought they would give me just the finishing touch I needed.

I rushed home and put on my makeup, filling in my eyebrows and broadening my eyes so that if you really squinted and Jackie was having a bad day, I looked like her very distant second cousin twice removed.

I then squeezed into my shoes and gown. I looked at the clock and opened the package of fingernails. The instructions on the package said I had to put some glue on first and then press on the nails. Instantly my hands were lovely. They had that look of never having seen a dishpan or a snow shovel. I practiced graceful poses in front of the mirror. Jackie, eat your heart out!!

This particular boyfriend, my date for the prom, was never on time. I always had to wait. But wouldn't you know men! Just when you want a little more time to be sure your nails are dry, then they show up on time! When the doorbell rang, I couldn't just leave him standing out on the doorstep. I grabbed my pearl purse and assumed a luscious smile and a soft whispery voice similar to Jackie's as she showed America the newly decorated White House.

When we arrived at the gym for the prom, there was a receiving line of dignitaries standing near the door. Dr. Nels Minne, the university president, waved when he saw me. As editor of the Winonan, the college newspaper, I had written a series of editorials supporting Dr. Minne in his university growth policies. The Minneapolis Tribune had quoted me, and I was one of his favorite students. He greeted me by taking both of my hands in his hands and squeezing enthusiastically.

I gulped and prayed that he didn't have a handful of fingernails stuck to his palm. He didn't look down at his hands as I introduced him to my date. Dr. Minne didn't seem to be aware that we had a sticky problem.

As my date and I walked away to dance, I looked at my Jackie hands that had looked so classy in the mirror a little earlier. A few nails were straight, but the rest were crooked--turned this way and that and every which way. I looked at Dr. Minne and saw that he was picking something off his hands. I think it was glue. Oh, Jackie......

Stealing from the Poor
by Marilyn Mikulewicz Baranski

The winters are long, and the snow is not for the weak of heart. A Minnesota sense of humor can help any of us survive those winters. Here's a story that always makes me chuckle.

The ladies from our church, St. Joseph's Catholic Church in Rosemount, were packing donated clothes for the poor of some foreign land in the world. They worked all day putting clothing in boxes, carefully folding items, pinning matching pieces together and finally closing the boxes and securing them with tape and rope. It was an all day job for a group of hard working church women.

Finally it was becoming dark as the sun goes down early in the dead of winter, and it was time to go home and prepare dinner for their families. The women started to put on their coats but, alas, Mrs. Mahowald's winter coat had disappeared. One look at the mound of sealed boxes told Mrs. Mahowald that her coat had been packed along with the donated clothes and was now headed out of the country. No one even cared that her house key and used handkerchief would be traveling with the coat.

As hard as the women had worked all day, no one was willing to reopen the packed boxes. So the women found another coat yet unpacked that fit her. Although Mrs. Mahowald wore the donated coat home, she was ashamed to wear it again as she feared someone would recognize it as the coat they had donated and think that Mrs. Mahowald, a good woman and a pillar of the church, had stolen from the poor.

Marilyn Mikulewicz Baranski earned her BS and MS from Winona State and taught and counseled high school students in Vallejo, California until 2003. Now retired, she does freelance writing and counseling, and she enjoys genealogy. She and her husband Fred have an adult daughter.

Zoo Sounds
by Marilyn Mikulewicz Baranski

Between the time I left home and when we went back to visit, the area had changed. The Twin Cities had grown out, covering the former farm land with housing developments and chain stores. The farms where my friends had grown up were now covered with very stylish homes. So many people had found the American dream back on those old cow pastures and cornfields.

I had heard of a new zoo that had been built close to our home-- within ten or so miles. I wanted to see what that land that I once knew looked like now that it was a zoo. The San Francisco Airport was fogged in again, and the airline offered us a later flight home, so we took advantage of an extra day in Minnesota.

My preteen daughter was excited because, I swear, next to "clothes," her first word had been "animals." At the first mention of zoo, she was ready. The Minnesota Zoo is located in Apple Valley, just west of Rosemount. The zoo was built in 1978 and is large, ever so clean, and spacious. As closely as possible, the animals are housed in their natural surroundings. It is really a neat place.

We strolled through the Tropics Trail, the Discovery Trail with its sharks and dolphins and the Minnesota Trail with native Minnesota animals that you never really see because they are underground, in the woods or are nocturnal. The zoo had cameras in the dens so that people could get an idea of what the animals did underground where people normally are never able to see. That was my favorite exhibit.

I was having a pretty good time at the Minnesota Zoo, and I really looked around to see if I knew anyone. I didn't seem to recognize anyone, but knew I would recognize someone at any minute. We went outside the lovely air conditioned building, and the heat hit in a way that only Minnesota heat can hit you on an August day. You literally stick to yourself and can't get a decent breath. I waved my hand in front of my face trying to create a breeze.

We looked at a few more outdoor exhibits and then decided to finish our zoo tour by taking a monorail trip around the rest of the 500-acre facility. I wasn't feeling well, as my hay fever had kicked in, coupled with the first day of a migraine headache. I wanted to continue though, as I didn't know when I would ever see the zoo again, and I wanted to see all of it.

We paid for our monorail tickets and were about to board when we saw a sign, "Quiet Car... No talking! No children!" Quiet and air conditioned! Boy, that was for me. I rushed onto that quiet car, and the air conditioned air engulfed my body. It was heavenly and so great. It was as good as a malted milk on a dry day. It was as good as a soft bed when your muscles hurt. It was...I don't know what else it was because that was when I was rudely poked and told to get off the train because the ride was over. Where was my ride? The person who poked me was my own child, the one to whom I had given birth after forty-some hours of labor--but that's another story. I had embarrassed her.

It seems that I had inadvertently fallen into a deep and sudden sleep. I sort of snored a little. To put it bluntly, as only my daughter could, I had "snored so loudly that the conductor had asked my daughter to waken me." Why did he want me awake? Because they had been broadcasting from the quiet car, and they wanted the quiet car QUIET because audio from that car was broadcast to eight other cars.

Eight cars full of zoo patrons had heard me snore. Eight carloads of people were trying to identify the new animal they heard over the loud speaker. Each time my daughter attempted to wake me, I had mumbled "Let Mama sleep."

She walked about 15 feet ahead of me as we left the zoo. You know how kids go through a stage when they don't want to admit who their parents are? They won't walk with you or be with you? That was the beginning of that stage. She didn't admit she was my child again until she wanted money. Was I embarrassed? Frankly, I was too tired to care. Did I ever meet anyone I knew? Not that I'm aware of. Then again, 30 years, a few extra pounds and a blast of wrinkles can make anyone unrecognizable in a crowd. Maybe I can go home again, and nobody will know that I was the one who fell asleep on the zoo train.........and snored a little.

Sailing Lessons
by Tom Bengtson

We lived in Minneapolis, just a few blocks from Lake Nokomis. Parkland surrounds the lake, and this was where we skated, rode our bicycles, played softball, and learned to swim.

Lake Nokomis had about 100 buoys for sailboats near its west shore. Boat owners rented buoys for the summer. Dad spent a lot of time looking at the boats, and so did I. The halyards, clanging against their masts, called like free samples at a candy store. I watched sailors rig their boats at the dock, taking note of their ropes and pulleys, mooring chains, cranks, hooks and stopwatches.

When we would go to Nokomis to play ball, I would always take a few minutes to check out the sailing area. During the week it was quiet, with the majestic scows floating on the mirror-like lake as if they were swans in a deep sleep. Most boats were protected by a canvas tarp, which prevented me from seeing inside the cockpit. Some were splattered with bird droppings, but the ones that protected against this hazard with a plastic owl perched near the top of the mast looked clean. I'd read the names across the transom: *Sunshine, Getaway, Lady Luck, Son of the Beach* and *Wet Dreams*.

Calypso was the name of a boat my friend sailed. Myron, the youngest of six children, lived across the street from Lake Nokomis, and his family owned a Johnson M Scow, a beautiful 16-foot boat with a jib and twin inboard rudders. Myron was one of my best friends from school, and during the summer between sixth and seventh grades, he took me sailing on the *Calypso*. Having sailed from infancy, Myron was a good sailor by the time he gave me my first ride on a sailboat. We rowed the tender to his boat, where I dropped him off and returned the rowboat to shore. In the meantime, he rigged the *Calypso* at its mooring and sailed it to the dock, where he picked me up. I sat near the front of the cockpit while Myron stepped off the dock and into the boat, giving us a little momentum to begin our reach across the lake.

Myron told me to watch out for the boom, the heavy beam that secured the bottom of the main sail. On the *Calypso*, the boom was made of wood and could easily have knocked an unsuspecting person unconscious. Myron let me control the jib, pulling and securing the appropriate lines on his command. He showed me how the boat responded to even slight movements of the tiller and mainsheet. I watched the painter off the bow flop in the water as we sailed and came about.

Most impressive to me was the way Myron could make the boat heel. With a certain wind, Myron could trim the mainsheet in such a way that the hull underneath us would rise out of the water. The boat was leaning over, and I thought we were going to capsize. As the hull rose, we arched back, locking our feet under the lip of the cockpit. We used our weight to counterbalance the boat, which seemed to be tipping into the water below us. The mast followed, reaching almost parallel to the water's surface. Sometimes Myron would let the mainsheet out a little, and the end of the boom would dip into the lake. I looked behind me and saw the bottom of the *Calypso*, the high-side sideboard protruding three feet into the air. It seemed nuts, but Myron knew what he was doing. We didn't capsize. We didn't even get wet. This was the thrill of sailing, pushing the limits of the boat and your skills. I thought it was fantastic, and I accepted every sailing invitation Myron ever extended.

***

One winter in the mid-1970s – I must have been about 14 -- Dad returned from the Boat Show and announced that he'd bought a sailboat.

He showed us a picture of the boat, which was called the *Wildflower*. It was black with a white deck and a big orange "W" on its mainsail. I had never seen a sailboat with a black hull before, but it looked sporty in the picture. The *Wildflower* was 12 feet long and shaped like a rowboat with a square bow. It was made of a kind of heavy-duty Styrofoam, and it had a teak bench with a centerboard through the middle. The aluminum mast reached probably 16 feet in the air, and there was a small jib. The picture showed the boat with a colorful spinnaker, but our boat didn't come with one.

Dad leased one of those Lake Nokomis buoys, and when spring came we prepared to launch our boat. We took about an hour to step the mast according to instructions; then we had to learn about rigging. It took another hour to figure out how to attach each of the sails and how to thread the ropes through the various pulleys. We were surprised by the buoyancy of the *Wildflower,* which sat remarkably high in the water, even with people in it. No more than a few inches of hull disappeared below the waterline. It was a relatively flat, wide boat, a design that seemed to accentuate the impact of Lake Nokomis' small waves.

Dad agreed to let me invite Myron on our maiden outing. We really didn't know how to sail, so it made sense to have Myron take us out. With the *Wildflower* rigged for action and tethered to the sailing dock, the Bengtson family of seven and Myron gathered for the inaugural voyage. Dad brought life preservers, the bright orange kind that wrap around your neck, significantly limiting the mobility of your head. Mom refused to get in the boat. Unable to swim, Mom had never liked boats much anyway, and the *Wildflower* appeared too unstable to fit within her comfort zone.

Five of us kids got into the boat. Three sat on the center bench and two sat near the mast, trying to stay out of the jib's way. Myron and Dad sat at the stern, where they had the best access to the tiller and mainsheet. After two hours of build-up, we had attracted a small crowd of strangers to watch our launch. Mom stood in the center of the group, arms folded, as she watched us take off. One of us in the boat lifted the painter over the dock post and pushed the bow toward the center of the lake. In an instant, wind filled our mainsail, and we started moving. Even with seven people in the boat, the *Wildflower* moved at a pretty good clip.

Myron tugged on the mainsheet and said he was going to "see what she could do." Dad urged caution, but Myron reassured Dad and got the *Wildflower* to heel. Water started to flow into the cockpit over a wide spot on the low side of the hull. Myron ignored it and kept pulling, trying to get the boat to heel even farther. But the *Wildflower* was not built like the *Calypso.* It was designed to sail on its belly, not on its side. We had been sailing only a few minutes when Myron passed the point of no return, and we began to tip. When Myron realized what was happening, he let go of the mainsheet, but it was too late. Once the *Wildflower* started to tip, there was no stopping her. The boat went over onto its side, the mainsail floating along the top of the water. Everyone fell into the cold water, although our life vests kept us floating. I caught a glimpse of my horrified mother on shore, her worst fears about sailing realized.

The *Wildflower* wasn't done yet. As the hull continued to take on water, the boat began to turtle. The mast disappeared into the lake, and the whale-like bottom of the boat rose out of the water. The mast was pointing straight down as our gloves, caps, and coins sank out of reach.

Dad frantically counted heads. He readily noted five bobbing figures, which was one less than he needed. "Where is Tom?" he thought. I had emerged in a cavity under the hull. No one could see me, but I had a unique view of the inside of the *Wildflower* with its rigging upset, its dagger-board falling in, and its tiller popping out of its mount.

A man on shore quickly rowed one of the tender boats and plucked all of us out of the water, including me after I swam out to where everyone could see me. Our rescuer returned the soaking kids to Mom, who took us to our car, where the heater prevented us from catching cold. Dad stayed to right the boat, a task that ultimately required the use of two tender boats. Although we were only about 25 feet from the dock, Dad said we were fortunate to be out far enough that the mast did not lodge in the lake's muddy bottom.

Despite the rocky start, sailing proved to be a wonderful hobby for Dad and me. Eventually, we figured out how to sail on our own. We learned how to reach and run and come about and jibe and cast off and land. By summer's end, I was slaloming around the buoys and the boats moored to them.

As a new sailor, I was intrigued by the way a sailboat gets from one spot to another. I learned that if you want to go from point A to point B, sometimes you have to sail toward point C for a little while. If my destination was directly upwind, I had to tack, the process of sailing in a zigzag pattern to get from a downwind spot to an upwind spot. The captain needs to figure out how many tacks to make and how steep to make each tack. Sailing races are won and lost on these decisions. In sailing, you have to work with nature; an experienced sailor knows that the path that seems obvious to the novice isn't always the best way to go.

Early October brought the end of the sailing season and the close of the best summer I had ever had. That funny little black boat was my ticket to the good life. I thought sailing was better than anything at school or my bike or Little League or even television. After helping Dad pack the boat away in our backyard for the winter, I asked him how many days until spring.

"Too many," Dad said. "Too many."

***

Two Boat Shows later, Dad came home with another announcement: "I have traded the *Wildflower* in for a new boat."

We rushed outside to behold a beautiful boat with a white hull and red deck. It was a 16-foot scow with a black aluminum mast and boom. A teak splash-break popped out of the deck just before the mast. Bailers on the floor of the cockpit promised to keep our feet dry, and the outboard tiller, with its aluminum extender, screamed for someone to take hold of her. The boat had just one sail, but what a sail! The mast was 24 feet high, and the sail curved outward to catch as much wind as possible. The flat-bottom hull with its two metal sideboards was designed for speed. This was a first-class boat that would roar through the water as fast as anything on Lake Nokomis.

As spring approached, I couldn't wait to put the new boat in the water. Dad named her *Rose Anne* over the objections of Mom, who said she was unlikely to ever take a ride in the boat. Nonetheless, Dad tenderly painted the name across the transom.

We opened the sailing season that year like we had before – in the community room at one of the city parks. Early each spring, the Minneapolis Park Board conducted a lottery for the buoys. During the winter, sailboat owners registered with the Park Board to get in on the drawing. As names were pulled from a hat, boat owners got to choose the buoy they wanted for the summer. If you didn't show up for the drawing, the Park Board gave you whatever buoy was left over at the end of the lottery--the ones farthest from the sailing dock. Dad and I considered the acquisition of a well-placed buoy to be absolutely essential to a good summer. Attendance at the lottery was very important, and we prayed that our names would be drawn early. On our way to the lottery that evening, neither of us said a word. Our fate lay before us, and there was nothing we could do about it.

We arrived to a crowded room, and the drawing soon began. The first name was announced, and it was not ours. The winner leapt out of his chair and raced up to the map displayed at the front of the room. The lucky sailor drove a pin through the best buoy on the lake – No. 1, located only a few feet from the sailing dock. His summer in paradise was set; he'd get all the benefits of a city lake mooring without much work. More names were drawn, and happy boat owners eagerly claimed their prize positions. Sometimes the moderator drew the name of a no-show. "He'll be sorry," my dad muttered just loud enough for me to hear.

Finally the man drawing names called, "Frank Bengtson." Dad and I rushed to the front of the room and selected a buoy in the middle of the pack. The one we got was far enough from shore that we wouldn't have to worry about fishermen casting into our boat, yet close enough that we wouldn't wear ourselves out rowing to and from our boat. With a decent buoy placement, I figured we could have a pretty good summer.

The *Rose Anne* proved easy to sail, and like Myron's boat, it was designed to heel. On a good run, the high side of the hull would rise out of the water, and the boat would pick up speed. I learned just how far I could push the *Rose Anne* before she would begin to lose speed and even tip over.

In fact, I eventually learned to tip the boat on purpose and right it by myself without getting wet. As the boat was going over, I'd climb over the high side of the hull and stand on the sideboard. My weight would reverse the momentum of the boat, and she would begin to right. As the mast came up out of the water, I'd climb back into the cockpit, my foot leaving the sideboard just as the hull would come crashing back on top of the water. Dad was so impressed by this little maneuver that he asked me to do it in front of the sailing dock, where he captured it on film with his Super-8 movie camera.

Sailing brought me life. The sound and smell of the lake water mixed with the warmth of the sun on my lean teenage body and made me high. A city lake is a wonderful place for a teen to be in the summer. How many people were watching the *Rose Anne* from shore, perhaps a little jealous? How many were looking at me, this kid who happened to be lucky enough to have a dad bit by the sailing bug? Maybe no one, in fact, but in my mind it was everyone, and I liked this celebrity status.

Although a sailor is completely dependent upon the wind, I found that a good afternoon of sailing actually has very little to do with the wind. I had fun regardless of whether the wind was whistling at 15 miles an hour or barely stirring. Apparently, it's not so much the power of the wind that matters but what you do with it.

I don't know if Dad ever realized how much his investment paid off for me. Sailing taught me at a young age lessons that I have carried with me all my life. You can't control the wind, and the best sailors don't complain about it. They focus on the things they can control, making adjustments that help make the most of their situation. Sometimes, a sailor encounters an unexpected shift in the wind that other sailors avoid. Yet, if you react to the shift correctly, it doesn't always slow you down. It may, in fact, prove to be just what you need.

Tom Bengtson, owner of a small publishing company and father of four children, lives in Minneapolis. "Sailing Lessons" is an adaptation from his memoir, "Emerging Son." Some of his other stories can be found at www.tMichaelB.blogspot.com. He hasn't sailed in years.

Pony Tails and Sandra Dee
by Betsy Hermanson

"Sandra Dee is dead." The news anchor read the information off his teleprompter with the same professional tones he used to describe war in Iraq, murder in Eagan, or other mayhem across the globe. Blah, blah, blah. It was the same old stuff, and I wasn't paying attention until I heard that name.

"What did he say?" I asked my husband. "Did he say Sandra Dee is dead? What did she die of?" (As if it made a difference) It was stunning news. Another icon is gone--another hero of my perfect life which was to be, which never came about, which never could have been.

Sandra Dee was my idol. When I grew into the magic age of teenager-dom, I wanted to be just like her--tiny, cute, with blonde hair sporting the perfect bouncy ponytail. It did not matter that at 13, I was already six inches taller than she, looked like my dad, and was constantly chided by my big sister about my big nose. At 13, I did indeed have a pony tail.

I worked hard for that pony tail. When we moved from a rural parsonage in Iowa to Mankato in 1957, I found I was hopelessly out of step with the world. I had never jumped rope and knew none of the rhyming verses the Mankato girls all recited. I rushed to learn, "I'm a Little Dutch Girl Dressed in Blue," but by then they had moved on to playing jacks, and never having been around concrete, I had never played jacks either. And even though I had clamp-on roller skates, I had never skated much because it's hard to roller skate on gravel. My girlhood had been spent climbing trees, playing house in the lilacs and corn crib, digging for Indian treasures in the cow pasture and riding down dusty gravel roads on my rusty red bike that I called Black Beauty.

I found a new best friend in Janet. One of the first things we found we had in common was that we each had pesky sisters three years younger and bossy sisters two years older. And although we loudly complained about those bossy older sisters, Janet Ingebretson and I secretly yearned to be just like them.

Mary and Margaret went to high school. One day we would too. They babysat regularly and had their own money for hamburgers and Cokes; we begged our mothers for change so we could walk down the Main Street hill and sit looking sophisticated in the Broiler Cafe while we sipped our frosty Cokes. They bought magazines; we borrowed them and read them from cover to cover. They wore girdles and complained about them pinching. We hoped that someday we would have something to pinch in too.

The main thing that labeled me as a country child and put Janet ahead with the other girls was that she had a lovely blonde page boy hairdo that she fussed with endlessly, while I was still in pigtails. When I stayed overnight at her house, Janet sat in front of her vanity mirror and clipped metal curlers into her hair so that her page boy would be curled softly towards her face in the morning. I wound one long braid or the other from behind my back around my arm and chewed on the end while I envied her beauty.

It wasn't fair. Not only was I tall, gawky and brown-haired, but my brown hair had never been cut. I looked like a freak, not like a stylish almost-teenager. There certainly weren't any Hollywood beauties in *Teen* Magazine who had such old-fashioned braids. In the morning, while Janet combed her fashionable locks, I splashed water on my wispy ends to flatten them down, and then like a baby, I went home to have my mother re-braid my hair.

I turned 12 in the spring of 1958 and was eligible to attend a week-long summer camp in Clear Lake, Iowa with some young people from my church. I wanted to go. Mary and Margaret were going, and Janet was going. Since she was a year older than I, she had gone last year, and she raved about the swimming, singing around the campfire, and roller-skating at a real rink with shoe skates.

I begged to go. I think the cost was $15, which didn't seem to be a problem for my folks. There was a big problem, however--my hair. Who would braid my hair? I would be gone for a week, and I couldn't take my mother along. I started to beg for something else. I wanted my hair cut.

My dad held out the longest. He liked my long brown braids. I guess he thought they kept me his little girl, but I was too big to be little. Finally he relented.

On a warm spring evening, my mother got out her sewing shears. They decided to take pictures first, and they had me dress up in my Sunday best. I unbound my hair, and Mom brushed it until it hung in braid-molded waves down my back past my hips. Then, perched on the kitchen stool where I had sat every morning for as long as I could remember while Mom braided my hair, I waited.

Mom, behind me as always, picked up scissors instead of a brush, and then she put them down. "Are you sure?" she asked. The whole family and a few neighbors were gathered around the kitchen for this big event, and they all stared, half in anticipation and half in fear that the show would not materialize.

"Yes, I want it cut," I said, never more sure of anything in my life. This was my stepping stone to freedom, my passage into adulthood, my chance to look like a normal human being. "Yes, I'm sure."

She picked up the scissors again and measured in several places up and down my back. Everyone had an opinion about where the cutting should begin. But I wanted a pony tail, so Mom began cutting a few inches below my shoulders. Quickly the deed was done. My head felt a lot lighter, and I swung my hair from side to side. Mom shed a few tears as she gathered the fallen tresses, rubber-banded them at the top, and braided them into a still-long braid. (I saved that braid for years, and even wore it as a hairpiece several times in high school and college.)

But now what? My hair, gathered into a pony tail, did not swing in bouncy curls as I walked. Instead, the thick stubborn locks formed a brown protrusion that sort of looked like a Christmas tree at the back of my head. Patiently my mom and sister worked with me to work with my hair. They bought me a bottle of Suave conditioner to tame the wildness and helped me clamp in rollers that were terrible to sleep on so that I could have curls in the morning. It was torture, but it was worth it. I would be a regular teenager.

Of course, I never was. Sandra Dee showed me that. As she bounced through *Gidget* and *A Summer Place*, I read magazines to find out how to be cute, perky and bubbly. A swinging pony tail didn't do it if you still tripped over your own big feet. A sassy mouth didn't do it when you were too shy to think of a retort until you were in bed at night, unable to sleep because of the bumpy rollers in the back of your head. But I dreamed and I hoped.

I went to camp in Clear Lake that summer, swam and sang around the campfire and roller-skated at the real skating rink. I only had to call upon Margaret once or twice to get me out of a fix with my pony tail. I faithfully followed Sandra Dee and the other starlets, but never became as much like them as I thought I would.

Once the deed was done and my first haircut was snipped, my hairdo gradually evolved over the next few years. I went through a perm, a razor-cut shag, and a Jackie bouffant after the braids were gone. But for one year, even if I didn't look the least bit like Sandra Dee, I was a teen-ager with a pony tail.

My last moments with
hip-length hair in 1958.

Betsy Hermanson and her husband Ross have lived in Wells for 30 years.
They have five adult children and two grandchildren.

St. Clair Drug, M.E. Roher, Prop.
by Dorothy Roher Schnackenburg

"St. Clair Drug, M.E. Roher, Prop." That's what the sign that hung in front of the store said. When I was little, I wondered what "prop" was.

My father graduated from the University of Minnesota College of Pharmacy in 1925, and my mother graduated from Winona Teachers College. In 1931 they bought the St. Clair Drug Store from Dr. Juliar and moved to town from Minneapolis. I'm not sure if the soda fountain was in the store when they bought it, or if it was a later addition, but it was probably the most popular spot in the store and also in the town. The St. Clair Post Office was located at the back of the store, and my mother and dad were the postmaster and postmistress. I remember Dad studying for his Civil Service exam, memorizing state capitals and other important facts for civil servants to know.

After their first day of business, they tallied their receipts and discovered that they had earned only five cents. There were only two doctors in town, Dr. Juliar and Dr. McBeth. The prescription business wasn't exactly thriving so Dad added many sidelines to make ends meet. He had a large veterinary medicine department; he sold wallpaper and would even go out and measure rooms for customers. He added a paint department, and he carried school supplies. In December, he added a good selection of Christmas gifts including toys, and I learned to gift-wrap when I was just a kid. Of course, Dad stocked regular drug store items and magazines. He also ran a small lending library.

Above the drug store we lived in a large three-bedroom apartment. It had a wonderful screen porch at the back. My sister Judy and I slept out there until the first snowflakes arrived. Cold!

Mother never made desserts. She'd say, "Go downstairs and get some ice cream." Ice cream is not one of my favorites to this day.

When I was in junior high, I was excused shortly before noon to go back to the store so I could work at the soda fountain during the noon rush. Malts cost 15 cents, milkshakes were 10 cents, and sodas, with two scoops of ice cream, also cost a dime. We made fountain Cokes and root beer in frozen mugs, and we made our own syrups. During the war, we had extra coupons for sugar so we could make simple syrup. When the town had free outdoor movie nights, our store would be swamped. It was lots of work, but fun too. Our soda fountain was the only one in a radius of 25 to 40 miles.

Labor Day was a big event in our lives. The drug store was closed, but we set up a hamburger stand right next door. My Uncle Donald, who was in high school in Stillwater, came every summer to work at our store. He was the fry cook at the Labor Day hamburger stand. Uncle Donald is now 88 years young, and he lives in Tempe, Arizona with his son.

In 1945, my dad, who was 40 years old, had gall bladder surgery at the Mankato hospital. Things went from bad to worse. His brother, Chris Rohrer, a doctor in Waterville, finally took him to the Mayo Clinic, where they literally saved his life. In January of 1946, with the war finally over, we were able to buy enough gas to drive to Prescott, Arizona. We stayed with my mother's sister while Dad fully recuperated.

The St. Clair Drug Store and its proprietor, M. E. Roher, in the '30s

During all the years in St. Clair, one or another of the Bollman girls worked at the drug store. I'm sure there were seven or eight sisters, but at the time we went to Arizona, I think it was Marie Bollman who held the store together, while a pharmacist buddy of my dad from Waterville came over a few times a week to help with prescriptions.

In Prescott my Dad became interested in a much bigger store. What had started as a rest cure in Arizona turned into a permanent move. My folks sold the store in St. Clair after a few months, and we moved all our stuff. My mother always wanted to move to Arizona, but she really missed St. Clair. With the help of a brother-in-law, my Dad bought the larger store. Uncle Donald got out of the service, earned a pharmacy degree at the University of Southern California, and joined my dad in his new store. They formed the Roher-Bloom Drug Store, and it was the perfect partnership. My dad got into Arizona politics and loved it. He was the chairman of the Yavapai County Board of Supervisors for 20 years.

My brother, sister and I graduated from Prescott High School. I went on to the University of Arizona and earned a degree in pharmacy. I couldn't get that drug store business out of my system. I don't know too much about what happened to the St. Clair Drug Store, but I don't think it remained a drug store for too many years after we left.

Dorothy Roher Schnackenburg lives in Carpinteria, California. She has eight children and 14 grandchildren, and she enjoys coordinating family events. She and her husband Bob enjoy spending time at their other house in Hawaii.

Berry Picking--A Family Affair
by Stella Hanson Sorbo

When we moved into the country close to Two Harbors, then to Silver Creek, and later to a place with the Stewart River in our backyard, neighbors helped me sleuth out berry patches nearby. Strawberry shortcake and jam were family favorites from my berry picking expeditions.

Our move to town did not deter my berry picking efforts. I found new patches and also returned to spots I'd found in my honeymoon days.

As our family grew, they were added to my berry picking crew. Days dawned clear or sometimes foggy in June or early July. Our daughters and I would gather up equipment that included plastic containers of various sizes and sometimes a picnic lunch. We'd pop the toddler into the wagon, or we would all walk down the sidewalks onto dusty Lighthouse Point Road and over the railroad tracks. To the left of the last tracks, in the tall grass of a little gully, we parked.

As we picked berries, we could view the dark, massive ore docks, weather-beaten boat and fishing houses hugging the shore, and the Edna G doing its chores. Cool Lake Superior breezes reached over the high grasses and welcomed us to our strawberry place.

"Oh, here are lots... these are mine... don't step on them. Come help me--there are too many for me to pick!" could be heard as the berry pickers got to work.

Sometimes little fingers got grass cuts or picked daisies that swayed tantalizingly back and forth in the wind. Lunch time was picnic and official rest time, and then maybe we went back to picking if we weren't too tired. We had red stained fingers, tired legs, and we smelled of sweet wild strawberries on our slow walk home.

Cleaning, or checking over cleaned berries, squishing berries for shortcake, and jam making came next for me. This is when I began to appreciate all the work my mom had done in canning. We enjoyed the fresh berries, and when winter came, the canned jam.

In later years, I discovered freezer jam recipes that were quicker and easier to make than canning. One is the delicious recipe of Nettie Buschena. Her recipe, "Very Best Strawberry Jam," is simple to make and always turns out. Here it is:

Combine three cups of strawberries and one-cup of sugar. Bring to a boil, and boil for three minutes. Add one more cup of sugar and boil for three more minutes. Add still one more cup of sugar and boil for three more minutes. Let the cooked mixture stand for eight hours or overnight. Put cold jam in jars and seal with paraffin. This jam also freezes well. If the berries are very ripe, add a little lemon juice to the recipe.

Stella Hanson Sorbo was born on a farm in Freeborn County. She is a teacher and freelance writer who lives in Two Harbors.

A Christmas Catastrophe
by Arthur Vogt

My most memorable Christmas was in 1930 when I was 8 years old. I wanted a yo-yo in the worst way because some of the older boys in school had yo-yos, and it fascinated me that they could make their yo-yos go up and down, sideways, around the world and even straight out. I thought it would be great if I could learn how to do all that.

I must have told the right people what I wanted, for sure enough, way down in the toe of my stocking was the most beautiful yo-yo I ever saw painted red, white and blue. I was ecstatic.

I tried to make my yo-yo do what I had seen the bigger boys do, but it wouldn't work for me. I tried to make it go down and up, but it didn't work. I tried to make it go around the world, and that was worse yet. Finally I was desperate, and I threw it straight out from me. The string slipped off my finger, and the yo-yo sailed out of the living room, through the kitchen and out the kitchen window. Unfortunately, it took the windowpane with it and landed in the snow. Now I was in trouble.

It was about 20 degrees below zero and about 5 o'clock in the morning. The noise of the breaking window woke my dad, and he got up. He got a hammer and some nails and some cardboard, and I had to hold the old kerosene lantern while he tacked cardboard over the broken window. I was scared and shivering and wondering what was going to happen to me, so I asked Dad if he was going to spank me.

He said, "No, this is Christmas." He put his hand on my shoulder and said, "I know you did not mean to do this, so let's go into the house and see if your mother has some hot chocolate and Christmas cookies so we can get warm.

I never got the hang of the yo-yo. My granddaughter knows how to do yo-yo tricks, and she's enjoyed hearing this story. Last Christmas, 74 years after this story took place, I found something in the toe of my Christmas stocking. It was a shining red yo-yo.

Arthur Vogt and his wife Maxine live in rural Kellogg,

The State School
by Kathy A. Megyeri

As the state plans for a new orphanage in Eagan, there is renewed interest in Minnesota's only state-run school for neglected children that closed its doors more than a half century ago in my hometown. My two aunts were dorm matrons at the state school, now called the Minnesota State Public School for Dependent and Neglected Children

I grew up in Owatonna, but the "state schoolers" as they were called, lived apart from the rest of the community on their self-sufficient campus. Between 1886 and 1945, 10,635 children lived there. The state school began as a working orphanage and closed because the social welfare system shifted to foster care. The formidable stone buildings housed classrooms, dormitories (called cottages) a gym with basement swimming pool, a nursery and hospital. It encompassed acres of field crops and housed farm animals. My parents referred to the orphanage as the "state school," but that's about all we knew of it. In reality, it took in children of troubled parents who signed rights to their offspring away to the state, but only 5 percent of its residents were orphans. Thirty-nine percent had one parent; 56 percent had two, but most children were abandoned.

One of its residents, Oscar Ronglien of Lakeville, remembers the hands-off visit through a screen with his tuberculosis-stricken mother. It was the last time he ever saw her. His father suffered from alcoholism and had a criminal record. Ronglien's brother Harvey remembers the day the two boys and their six older siblings were lined up in front of the county courthouse in Benson to be given away. He recalls, "If anyone wanted one of us, they just came and got 'em. Finally, we were the only ones nobody took." Then 4 and 6, he and Oscar were too young to work, so they joined 500 other hard-luck kids at the school.

The children lived in sixteen cottages; girls filled four of them and boys lived in twelve. Each housed 35 or more children and was tended by a lone "matron" 24 hours a day, every day. The youngsters rose early and went to bed at 7:30 every night, even in summer. On Sunday mornings, they attended a church service. My one aunt, Louise Rahm, never had any children of her own and was a widow, so being a matron suited her lifestyle, but she never cracked a smile, possessed no mothering skills, and thrived on regularity. Even in her later years, she followed the schedule of the state school: Monday was wash day, Tuesday, she ironed, Wednesday, she baked, Thursday, she sewed and mended, Friday, she marketed, Saturday, she cleaned, and Sundays were always reserved for church and prayer meetings. At the state school, Louise saw to it that her girls cared for the toddlers and infants kept in the nursery. They daily washed, peeled, and chopped vegetables grown on the premises and canned them in season.

My other aunt, Erma Kriesel, was the opposite of Louise; fortunately, she was a matron in a boys' cottage. She was a large woman, read voraciously, didn't follow such a set schedule, had innate intelligence and an inquiring mind, and loved her "boys." They worked in the fields, barns and in the massive dining room, where they scrubbed the tile floor three times every day, and on Saturday they had to clean the cottage floors with wool rags while on their hands and knees. Frequently, one or two would complain to Erma about being whipped in the fields by the school's hired men if they pulled weeds too slowly, but she was a kindly matron, and as long as the work got done, she preferred reading to the young ones and comforting the older boys.

Although both my aunts have died, their photos with their charges hang in the entrance hall to the state school. The main building now houses a museum, started by former student Harvey Ronglien, now the acting historian. His 90-minute documentary film, *The Children Remember,* was financed primarily by grants from the Minnesota Historical Society.

In the movie, Arlene Nelson of Owatonna retells an experience that her mother, Sara Etta Richards, told after she helped new students survive the ritual of admittance to the school. Because head lice were common with youngsters living in such close quarters, Sara had to help pour kerosene through newcomers' hair to keep the lice out of the cottages. She recalled a 3-year-old who put up such a fuss that they could not hold him down. A matron was called to help, but the child died from drowning in the kerosene while Sara was holding his arms. She never got over that experience.

According to school records, 198 children died at the school of injuries, pneumonia, measles, smallpox, tuberculosis, diphtheria, diarrhea, drowning or "wasting away." A cemetery at the rear of the school attests to their loss, and originally 151 graves were marked with only a number on a cement slab. Curator Harvey Ronglien, with the help of the community, replaced the slabs with wooden crosses that bear each child's name.

Former students remember that rules were harsh and firm. Students in the video remember that matrons and other authority figures had short fuses and no qualms about corporal punishment. Eugene Bliss of Austin vividly recalls a run-in with the school's first and longtime superintendent, Galen Merrill. "He just clapped one ear and busted my eardrum because I was naughty."

Lester Felien of California remembers a cottage matron who whipped him with a brush on his bare backside because he talked in bed. Eva Carlson Jenson of Owatonna remembers a staff member striking her for crying soon after she arrived. "I was sobbing because I missed my family," she says. "The matron said, 'We don't cry around here,' so I kept my sobbing inside."

Helen Hoover Bowers of St. Paul recalls a lack of affection or approval. "You never heard, 'You did a good job,' or 'It's good to have you here,' or 'We care for you,' not to mention an 'I love you'."

These former students, who are now in their 60s, 70s and 80s, remember having to learn to show affection and think for themselves. Harvey Ronglien says, "We were treated like robots but never learned about family structure. I had to learn what a cousin, an aunt, and an uncle were. As an adult, I had to learn about relationships."

But the survival skills they learned stayed with them. Vivian Swan Manthe from Dallas says, "The school saved my life…really saved my life." The girls learned to clean, cook, bake and sew. The boys learned farm work, and as teenagers, many were assigned to live and work on neighboring farms while they continued to go to school. Some said they had more education than their siblings who were taken in by families.

Only 4% of the children were ever adopted. Most left the school because they were put out on indentured contracts to work on farms or in homes. Ronglien, who came to the school at age 4, stayed until he was 16.

While he was still a ward of the state, a St. Paul family who worked as custodians and in the laundry of Miller Hospital employed Harvey on an indentured contract, but Harvey couldn't adjust to being there and ran away. He returned to Owatonna and stayed with four others in a rooming house as he worked his way through high school doing part-time jobs at the Owatonna Tool Company. On his 18th birthday, he enlisted in the Army, and after two years, returned to finish high school in Owatonna. He worked at Gopher Athletic Supply and then joined the Owatonna Utilities as a first class lineman, and retired from there after 30 years.

Oddly enough, Harvey heard from the local gas station owner that a couple of former orphans came back to see the place where they had spent their early years, but were told, "What state school? There wasn't one here." Newcomers to Owatonna had either not known of the place, were never told of its existence, or thought those grand old buildings on the west side of the city had always housed city and county offices.

Determined that the state school not be forgotten, Harvey and his wife Maxine visited radio and TV stations to solicit funds for an on-site memorial and museum. With the help of businesses and the community, they have established a tribute to those who worked and lived in the "orphanage," as many still call it. If only my aunts were alive to add their recollections to the museum's history. Their stern unsmiling faces standing alongside their charges tell only part of the story of life at the state school, and Harvey and his classmates are attempting to tell us the rest.

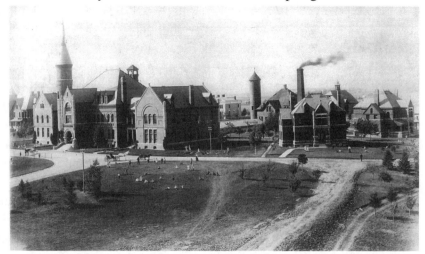

Minnesota State Public School for Dependent and Neglected Children, Owatonna

A Fly-In Fishing Vacation
by Kathy A. Megyeri

My mother was an avid fisherman. Growing up near Minnesota lakes, she knew the intricacies of bait and tackle. She even talked my dad into ice fishing on Lake Bemidji, where they rented an icehouse for three days. Dad remembers holding on to her in high winds while climbing into the wooden shack and catching nothing but those black, evil-looking eels that are such a delicacy in France. After that, they confined their fishing outings to the summer months. One year, Mother heard that the walleye were really biting in Canada. Since her favorite northern Minnesota lakes were getting "fished out" and the new owner of a fishing camp called Moose Point Lodge was offering a special to acquaint Minnesotans to the ultimate vacation—a fly-in week of fishing at a very remote spot--she was immediately hooked.

I did not accept my parents' invitation to join them enthusiastically because I had never fished. As a youth, I had wiggled out of going with my parents because I hated baiting the hook with earthworms, hated removing the hook from the jumpy fish, and hated cleaning the scales off even more. I always found an excuse to visit Grandma instead. I also knew that Canada would be cold, even in August, but my husband and I arrived in Minneapolis determined to be good sports, mostly because Mom volunteered to pay for our week's vacation. My husband was more game than I--flying into the wilds of Canada in a float plane toward Hudson Bay would be a new experience and one he might actually enjoy. So joining my parents, we traveled 380 miles or five hours by car from Minneapolis to International Falls and across the border to Fort Frances, Ontario.

After spending the night at a charming hotel named La Rendezvous, with a dining room overlooking Rainy Lake, we drove east on Highway 11 at 5 a.m. to the Northern Wilderness Outfitters. There we boarded a 1946 DeHavilland Otter float plane for our one hour, twenty minute (140 mile) trip northeast to lake Shikag, which means "skunk" in Ojibwa.

Each passenger is allowed 80 pounds of luggage including tackle box and poles, but the four of us and our cargo took very little space. However, the plane's hull was nearly filled with cases of beer, pop, and food. Everything--gas, fuel, outboard engines, lumber, minnows—has to be flown in to camp, and a thorough weights and balance check for the airplane must be completed before departing. The Otter seats eight comfortably, and the bush pilot provides earphones to help protect those on board from engine noise. Passengers wear jackets because cabin temperatures are not easily adjusted. Flying approximately 1500 feet over blue lakes and jade green forests takes the traveler far away from traffic jams and everyday routines in a matter of minutes, but seeing forests being decimated by logging crews from the airplane's windows is a most disheartening sight.

Deplaning at our Moose Point Lodge destination, 60 air miles from the nearest civilization, we scanned the outgoing guests' faces for happy smiles and successful fishing stories. They admitted the catch had been only fair, as it had rained steadily most of the week. All were men, all were avid outdoorsmen, all shopped Cabella's religiously as evidenced by their equipment and clothes, all admitted they were out of beer, but all still swore that this camp was the best.

Moose Point Lodge offers no amenities like TV or room radios. A huge wood-burning stove heats its one main log cabin lodge. Stuffed fish and mounted fox and wolf heads decorate the walls. The communal dining room consists of worn wood tables and chairs. Our news of the outside came from our Indian guides who listened to their own radios at night, mostly for Minnesota Twins baseball scores.

After a breakfast of pancakes and waffles, we met our guide, "Hog," an Ojibwa Indian from the nearby Couchichino Reservation. As a youth, Hog was in and out of scrapes with the local police and was frequently incarcerated until he paid his fines or sobered up, which usually occurred yearly near February 2. When the townspeople regularly saw him emerge from jail, they likened him to Punxsutawney Phil of Groundhog Day fame and labeled him Hog.

Hog was amicable, kind and capable. He escorted two of us on board a large, clean, well-maintained, aluminum fishing boat that contained two seats with backs, an ample gasoline supply, a snack and beverage container, a keeper of bait, and a new, dependable, fifteen-horsepower Yamaha engine. Within minutes, Hog had baited our hooks with minnows and "jigs," colorful metal weights attached to our hooks.

During the next half hour, we landed two walleyes, the most sought-after catch on Lake Shikag. Hog was able to find the best fishing areas, pull fish on board with the help of his net, monitor the engine, bait hooks, unravel tangled fish lines, determine each fish's weight, pose for photos, tell wind direction, and sense the needs and desires of his clients. Truly he was an amazing man. At 59 years of age, he had guided fishermen for 30 years. I learned to respect and admire these Indian guides who so calmly and patiently wait on us tourists, city slickers, and for the most part, Golden Gopher lovers.

We fished with success until noon, when Hog announced that we had enough "keepers" for lunch and pulled ashore on a sandy beach. He cleaned and deboned our five keepers, fetched the portable Coleman stove from under his boat seat, and extracted a container of homemade bread, onions, pickles, and a can each of spaghetti, beans, corn and pears. He also produced silverware, plates, and a fry pan. In no time, Hog made "mud" (coffee) for each of us, dipped walleye fillets in Aunt Jamima pancake mix, fried them in hot shortening, and made the most delicious fresh fish sandwiches I had ever tasted. For dessert, we had canned fruit and homemade cookies with more mud, beer or pop. Then everyone rested or sneaked a couple of feet away into the forest for a "bear squat."

Hog told us that Lake Shikag has over 100 miles of scenic shoreline on five interconnected lakes. Its depth and bottom structure are most important for catching fish. With an average depth of 20 feet, there are no large, deep sections where fish can hide in the warmer months of July and August. The bottom structure of Lake Shikag consists of sand and gravel bars with countless reefs and shoals. These two features, depth and bottom structure, make great spawning grounds and ensure plentiful fish reproductions. These features are why guides are not necessary, but my mother was convinced we'd get lost on this large lake if we fished without one. She had tried fishing on Vermilion Lake without a guide and was unsuccessful.

For the most part, fishing remains good not only in May and June, when the resort is filled, but also in July and August, when the weather begins to cool. We wished we had dressed in lightweight underwear under our blue jeans and rubberized rain gear, but about noon, we started to shed clothing and were grateful we had "layered" the way our Indian guides do. Most wear flannel wool shirts under their rain gear, worn more to cut the wind than to fend off unexpected showers. Duck shoes or hiking boots keep the feet dry and warm. With wind, sun, and waves, sunglasses and a good hat are a must, no matter how inexpensive or fashionable the rest of the outfit.

After lunch, it was back into the boat and on to more fish. The guides refer to northerns as "snakes," but they like to keep the large ones that tourists don't want for themselves to eat over the winter months. The guides claim there is little difference in taste between the coveted walleye and the less desirable snake, once filleted and fried, but most seasoned fishermen argue with that contention. Northerns prey on small walleye and seem almost easier to catch, although they fight the hook with more enthusiasm. The walleye is known as an elusive fish; less aggressive, it may spit out the bait or minnow. Some fishermen even like the lake trout and small mouth bass fishing that's available. Walleye and small mouth bass average two to three pounds, so it's a matter of preference.

I learned the key to catching fish is setting the hook. When I felt a slight tug, I let my pole trail closer to the water until the walleye had tasted my minnow; then I yanked on the pole to set the hook into his mouth and gently reeled him up to the side of the boat where Hog was waiting with the net. After a couple of hours, I could even tell the difference between a walleye and "snake," and if a walleye, its size. A small "wiggler" (under one and half pounds) would be thrown back. Because my idea of a perfect vacation is the five-star Greenbrier Resort in West Virginia, I was thrilled that Hog detached each catch from the hook, put it on the keeper line which dangled alongside the boat, and even baited my hook with minnows. What a luxury!

Hog told us at 4:40 that it was time to head back to camp, and we marveled that a day's fishing could be over so soon. At 5, we were back at camp, where Hog cleaned our three "snakes" and twelve walleye, our limit of six each to be frozen and taken home. Hog wrapped the fillets and labeled them.

Suppers of meat, not fish, were served at 7 every evening, so we had two hours to lounge around camp, walk up and down the small beach, play horseshoes, have a cocktail, compare fish stories, repair tackle boxes and lines, and meet other guests. We learned that most were Twin Cities folks who had tired or outgrown Lake Mille Lacs, Red Lake and Leech Lake. They had better luck in Canada and more bragging rights after a trip to Lake Shikag. My parents, husband and I were the only newcomers; most had been coming for years for an average of four days of fishing each summer. Some stayed for a week or more.

After dinner, some guests played cards or chatted, but we listened to Hog play his guitar, while our waitress Michelle sang "Oh Canada," as she does for winter hockey games at her school. Ted Davis, the owner, related camp stories while his wife, Faye, baked fresh bread, part of the hearty camp chow. Potatoes, vegetables and fruit arrive via float plane from International Falls or are portaged in from nearby Indian encampments, and I appreciated the menu-planning.

Most of us, unused to being on the water for eight hours, were glad to shower and go to bed at 10. Guests were considerate of each other, and only an occasional snore was heard until Ted blew his horn for 6:30 reveille. Breakfast was promptly served at 7. Our room with twin beds, linoleum floor and a bathroom was neat and clean. We would have booked a small outside cabin, with two bedrooms and two baths, but those three accommodations were taken first. Moose Point's capacity is only 30 people, and workers must commit to an entire summer away from home. Space aboard the float plane stays reserved for guests and supplies.

Never dreaming I would become an avid fisherman like my mother, I got hooked by this vacation get-away that totally disengages the mind from a daily routine. My husband, a workaholic, admitted that he had not thought of his office once. The word "wilderness" took on new meaning for the two of us, so accustomed to high-density living and traffic. I learned to admire the intimacy of our Indian guide's relationship with nature. Best of all we brought back our frozen walleye in a small cooler and fried them in beer batter for supper that fall, pleasant reminders of our fly-in Canadian fishing trip north of the Minnesota border.

Kathy Megyeri, the co-founder of the "Minnesota Memories" series, lives in Washington, D.C., writes for the CHICKEN SOUP books, and is an education consultant. She can be contacted at Megyeri@Juno.com.

First Holy Communion, Confirmation, and the Pledge
by Lauretta Lynch Cords

My mother died when I was an infant, and my aunt and uncle in St. Clair raised me as their own. My dad lived in another town, and I saw him whenever we could arrange a visit.

I loved going to catechism at Immaculate Conception Catholic Church in St. Clair. The pastor, Father Kiley, taught us well, making our religion clear and interesting. As we approached First Holy Communion, we were instructed not to be thinking of the pretty clothes we were wearing, but of the occasion. The boys wore knee-length pants and white shirts with ties; the girls wore white dresses, white veils and a wreath of waxed flowers on our heads. With all this finery, we had a lot not to think about.

We were told not to talk excessively, laugh, or act in a frivolous manner that morning, or even all that day. I tried very hard to carry out these instructions from the moment I got up on that first communion day, August 15, 1910. My father had sent me a lovely dress made of white albatross material, which was popular at the time. It was difficult not to look at it once in awhile or maybe to feel a little vain or to admire myself. This may have happened to some of the others too, but at least the effort was there, and I think the Lord generally looked upon us with favor.

About a year later, we were confirmed, so that meant another summer of extended instructions. The lessons now were longer and much harder, involving much serious study. Father Kiley wanted us to be ready to answer any question the bishop might ask. My aunt bought my confirmation dress, made of a pretty voile material with wide lace insertions. At this time it was just beginning to be possible to buy some quite nice ready-to-wear clothes.

Our class was very concerned about confirmation day, particularly what questions would be asked and by whom. Everyone was not questioned by the bishop himself, although Bishop Heffron was a very kind man. The bishop stood behind the altar railing and was flanked by two priests on either side. We formed a line of about ten in front of this group, and each received a question from one of them, after which another line would move up.

We were especially afraid of Father Trainor from Waseca because if you didn't answer him correctly he was likely to bawl you out in front of everybody. So when my line came up, the first thing I did was try to figure out who would question me. It turned out to be Father Coleman from St. Mary's.

When my turn came, the priest must have sensed this shy little girl, looking scared and hoping and praying I could have the strength to answer--if I knew the answer. So this kindly priest leaned forward and, putting one hand on the altar railing, asked me confidentially, and in a low, clear voice, "What is sanctifying grace?"

I leaned forward and answered very confidentially and in a low and perhaps not so clear voice, "Sanctifying grace is that grace which makes the soul holy and pleasing to God." I remember he smiled at me and nodded and said, "Good girl."

Father Kiley was very helpful that day too. He stood back on the altar and tried to remind some class members of answers they did know, and inform a few of answers they didn't. For example, if the question called for the number of commandments, he would hold up ten fingers. On more difficult questions, he would form the answers with his lips.

When you were confirmed, you had to take the "Pledge." You raised your right hand and repeated after the bishop that no liquor of any kind would pass your lips until you came of age. This was serious business, and I raised my hand somewhat reluctantly as it meant no tasting of the good grape wine that my aunt made, to say nothing of the more potent dandelion wine. Also ruled out was the small glass of beer I enjoyed on a hot summer's day when my uncle bought a pony of it to serve to the hired men on special work occasions.

That summer my father came to get me for a visit, and thinking I was too thin, he prescribed a glass of beer a day to increase my appetite. He owned a saloon so he had plenty of beer. Well, I had to tell him about the "Pledge," and when I did, he about hit the ceiling. He said, "I guess it won't hurt you to have a little beer. The Pledge is for older people who can't stop drinking."

This was a real problem for me because I had been instructed that I would surely go to hell if I broke the Pledge. But I did have some beer at my dad's place. Then there was the delicious beer soup that Auntie made for me when I was sick with the flu. It supposedly had special healing properties, but it posed another problem.

After all these years, I still occasionally feel guilty for having broken the Pledge, and I fear that I'll have to answer for it in the next world. I hope my father will be there to help bail me out, and that Auntie will also be there to offer a big bowl of her beer soup to St. Peter.

Lauretta Lynch, age 5

Lauretta Lynch Cords married Arthur Cords in 1922 and raised three children, Betty, Nick and Joan, in St. Clair. She moved to the Twin Cities after her husband's death, and she wrote her memoirs three years before she died in 1980.

Art Cords, Mr. St. Clair
by Nick Cords

On the day of his funeral, April 6, 1963, as all the businesses in town closed, I believe it was Stan Drake who referred to Art Cords as Mr. St. Clair. In such a small, close-knit town, I'm sure many of that generation of businessmen would qualify for the title along with Art. But because he was my father, and given that particular moment in time, I'm sure the reader won't mind if I vigorously endorse Stan's choice for the title.

Arthur Oscar Cords was born on June 4, 1898, to John and Clara Cords, who farmed a modest sized farm at the outskirts of St. Clair. Art, his preferred nickname (as opposed to Artie, my mother's choice), had two older brothers, Erwin and Vernie, and two younger sisters, Daisy and Viva. Erwin, Vernie and Viva preceded Art in death.

Art stayed at home to help on the farm, as Vernie, for example, took up a wandering and sometimes exciting life. Farming was difficult in those horse-reliant years, and especially under the Teutonic taskmaster that John was. Clara, however, kept the rigors of life from being too strenuous by providing a sensitive buffer between father and son.

Art left school sometime during the seventh grade, arguing that he was needed at home, but that may well have been an excuse, as it was for so many others. About this time, against all the good advice of Professor Harold Hill in *The Music Man*, he began hanging out at the local pool hall, which was then located in the rear of the barbershop. Soon he was racking balls for the older players, and actually shooting pool in his spare time. Here he found a hidden talent, and soon he was collecting fees and playing for the house. In his late teens, he actually played for the house in the largest public pool hall in St. Paul. Homesickness, however, brought him back to St. Clair to take up another of his interests--barbering.

During his time at the local pool hall, he had started lathering customers' faces prior to the barber shaving them, and then he started to shave, and then, under careful tutelage, to cut hair. Subsequently he became a licensed barber and with various partners, took over the barbershop, which still included the pool hall.

Another reason Art returned to St. Clair was his growing interest in Lauretta Lynch, whom he married on October 12, 1922. They had three children: Betty Marie (1925), Nicholas John (1929) and Joan (1931). He was a devoted husband, father and family man, an exemplary role model at home and a pillar of the community.

During his 40+ years as a barber, the shop became and remained one of the central forums for taking up and debating the great issues facing St. Clair and the world. The other forums were the liquor stores, where debates were a bit more exciting, but less clear. Dad served the community in many informal and formal capacities, and he was president of the Commercial Club for several terms.

After suffering a heart attack in 1951, he couldn't return to work for nearly nine months. He was able to continue at his beloved barbershop for twelve more years, plagued with occasional health setbacks. Fittingly, he died on the streets of St. Clair, suffering a fatal heart attack on the sidewalk near his property two months before his 65th birthday and possible retirement. Father Hodapp, a good friend, celebrated the Mass of Christian Burial at the Immaculate Conception Catholic Church. Art lies buried in the adjoining cemetery with his wife Lauretta. Along with other deserving past, present and future contenders, this Mr. St. Clair, Art Cords, justly remains in cherished memory.

Art Cords in his St. Clair barber shop

A Musical Boyhood in St. Clair
by Nick Cords

My musical life derived no doubt from a certain amount of inherited ability, and more important, from growing up in a musical environment. My mother, Lauretta (Larie) Cords, emanated maternally from a very musical German family, the Pestkas. Her father, although certainly not as musically oriented, at his wedding reception is said to have danced a jig on a red-hot stove top without charring his shoes. Yes, Nick Lynch was Irish--and a saloon keeper and wit for good measure.

My father, Arthur Cords, was not musically talented certainly in the sense Mother was. His claim to any artistic fame was while using only the index finger of each hand, he could play "Peter, Peter, Punkin' Eater" on the piano, with gloves on--after a few drinks. He was, however, extremely supportive--at times perhaps tolerant--of the rest of the family's musical shenanigans.

Mother, who received lessons from an early age on the organ and piano, was a very good player, and many joyous, if not perfectly harmonious evenings were spent with the Pestkas and others around the Hallet-Davis piano singing old songs. And they all helped form the Catholic Church choir for a time, with Mother playing the organ on Sundays.

Although St. Clair (population 350) was not Mozart's Salzburg or even Louis Armstrong's New Orleans, it was most certainly not lacking in musical opportunities. The author Bill Holm has said, "The heart can be filled anywhere on earth," and that was musically true for me in St. Clair.

By the time I was 5, I had embarked on a public music career of sorts as a boy soprano, thanks largely to the gentle urging of Mother. I performed with the McComb Sisters' Acrobatic and Variety Show; my featured show stopper involved singing the current Al Jolson hit, "About a Quarter to Nine." I was supremely devastating, at least according to the McComb sisters, Shirley and Capitola, and Mother. My sister Betty and Jeanette Nyquist performed an acrobatic dance in the show.

Barbara Maxon was another producer type who engineered various entertainment delights in St. Clair. The most personally memorable of these was a couple's performance of "Ma, He's Makin' Eyes at Me." At the performance, on cue from Bob and unbeknownst to the girls, the boys kissed their partners, and thus I got to kiss Margie Timmerman. I don't know about Margie, but I loved it.

I sang leads in nearly all the school Christmas operettas while continuing my boy soprano career. My last hurrah came in November of 1939, following the Nazi and Russian invasions of Poland. At a patriotic rally held in the St. Clair Town Hall, I sang Irving Berlin's "God Bless America" in about the same key and timbre as Kate Smith.

My high voice was deserting me, but other musical interests had arisen. At age 8, to fill the void left by utter failure at the piano, I took up the guitar and almost overnight became a singin' cowboy and yes--a yodeler to boot. Along with Jimmy Fitzloff, I actually took guitar lessons from Irv, the yodeling cowboy. In truth, and in defense of Irv, he was a schooled musician as well as a very good teacher. He taught me to read chord symbols so I could wail on the likes of "When It's Lamplightin' Time in the Valley." On Saturday nights my corral was "The Grand Old Opry" whenever I could ace my sister Betty out of listening to "Your Hit Parade."

In Fifth grade, a new wonder appeared in my musical world: the slide trombone. A local trombonist, Reed Macomber, directed the St. Clair summer school band, and when he asked what I wanted to play, I moved my right arm out and back, as I'd seen Reed himself do. The instrument became almost literally the center of my life, aided and abetted by the fact that I was quite good at playing it. It was the big band era, and Tommy Dorsey quickly replaced Roy Acuff as my idol.

Along with playing in the St. Clair School band, and thanks mainly to Harold Boswell, I played my first dance job at age 14 at Elysian with the Clete Fredericks Orchestra. The World War II manpower shortage no doubt helped me get started that young. I continued to take trombone lessons from the school band director Heinie Udelhofen, Ray Saunders and Jack MacKay, principal trombone with the Minneapolis Symphony. I played a trombone duet with Heinie at my high school graduation in 1947.

After high school, I played in an Army band and then majored in music and history at Mankato State College. I worked my way through college by playing in Spike Haskell's Jolly Millers Orchestra and continued dance work several years beyond that. After college, I actually taught public school music until I switched to teaching history, which became my permanent profession.

I continue to play avocationally, with the Century College Concert Band and the White Bear Lake Unitarian Society Jazz Ensemble. Our family, including my wife Maggie and my sons Jim, John, Nick and Dan, has been and remains deeply involved with music. Nick and Dan are professional musicians.

My life indeed has been highly enriched, even blessed, by music, and it all began and was nurtured during my boyhood in St. Clair--my personal Salzburg, my personal New Orleans.

White Bear Lake resident Nick Cords taught high school history and humanities in Albert Lea before moving on to Century College, where he taught for 26 years. Now retired, he enjoys reading, writing and playing trombone for tolerant and sometimes unsuspecting audiences.

Cars, Trucks and Terraplanes
by Lloyd Deuel

I was born in 1929, and I started driving cars in the 1930s and was licensed to drive in the mid 1940s. Most of the cars that I started driving were old.

My dad, Ira Deuel, bought his first car in 1923. He worked all winter logging near the Deuel farm. When he was paid off in the spring, he spent his earnings of $375 on a new 1923 Ford Model T, considered the best car on the road at the time.

This car needed cranking to start. There were rigid rules on the correct method to crank any car, but they were not always heeded. Cranking was right-handed and almost impossible for left-handers. One had to step with right foot over the bumper, engage the crank so that it could be pulled a quarter turn up with the cranker's thumb on the same side of the handle as the four fingers. The crank engaged on a ratchet principle so that it would disengage when the vehicle started. If, for some reason, it didn't start and backfired, the crank would pull backwards, and if the thumb was wrapped around the handle, the backwards pull would severely injure the cranker--often breaking his arm at the elbow.

I witnessed my dad cranking the Foreston Fire Department Buick fire truck when he cranked incorrectly (like he warned us not to do). The crank came out of position and spun around his head while still in his hand. The knob end hit him on the forehead and knocked him unconscious.

My wife Phyllis, while walking home from church with her parents, witnessed a man cranking his car. He broke his arm and suffered other injuries as they were passing by. This man later died from the cranking injury. It was not unusual to see a man with his right arm in a cast from an injury suffered while cranking a car, truck, or farm tractor.

Another quirk of old cars was that they had mechanical brakes, as hydraulic brakes did not appear until the mid 1930s. Mechanical brakes worked somewhat if they were in good repair, which was seldom. When

I learned to drive, these cars were older, and during Depression years, money was sparse and not spent on auto tune-up. When braking, one had to stomp the pedal to the floorboard. I learned that mechanical brakes were almost like no brakes, and stomping on the brake pedal seemed to make the car go faster. The modern day expression "pedal-to-the metal" was borrowed from the brake pedal of old cars rather than the gas pedal.

Drivers of these first cars compensated for the lack of good brakes by driving very slowly. The only roads that were paved were the state roads, and the county and township roads were gravel and rutted, and slow driving was a necessity.

Ford came out with the Model A in 1927. A big improvement over the Model T, it was faster, had a regular transmission and shifting lever, and proved to be nearly indestructible. It could navigate muddy roads, deep snow, and would always start easily. Faster speed became a problem because the car still had mechanical brakes. Many Model A cars lasted until after World War II, when automotive companies started building cars again.

My Grandpa Deuel bought a purebred Percheron stallion in 1922. He had learned to service a stallion from his stepfather, Tink Cone. He in turn taught my dad how to service this stallion. Horses were the mainstay of farming up to this time. The state had rigid laws governing stallions as an attempt to improve the quality of the horse population. The owner had to keep records on all breeding done by his horse and had to keep a stud-book available for inspection. The bloodlines were to be adhered to.

My dad built a two-wheeled chariot type of cart that was pulled by the stallion, Jerome. He drove Jerome to the neighboring farmers in Milo Township to service their mares. Jerome proved to sire outstanding foals, and his reputation spread. The cart proved to be too slow as the radius traveled from home became wider.

Dad bought the stallion from Grandpa for $1,000 and bought a Ford Model T truck in 1926 to transport him. The service fee for Jerome was $2 at the time of service and an additional $8 the next year if there was a standing foal when my dad came around with Jerome for the next service. A new legal studbook was started each year to comply with the law. The studbook contained the foal's date of birth, a description of both mare and foal, and if the owner paid the $8. Jerome was serviced for 17 years, and most of the studbooks showed entries of between 90 and 100 mares each year.

Dad's Model T truck was a 1-ton truck touted to carry a 2-ton load because it came with a Warford Auxiliary 6 speed transmission. This truck was considered the very best when it was new in 1923, and it sold for slightly under $600. It did come with a starter. The diagram that I saw showed five pedals on the floor, two of which were brake pedals and three were for the clutches. The gas was regulated from the steering wheel, as was the spark. My dad thought he had the ideal mode for transporting his stallion.

One drawback was the high platform rack on this truck, which made the center of gravity very high. A 1900-pound draft horse stands high, and his center of gravity is high. Together the center of gravity for horse and truck was dangerously high. If my dad drove slowly and the road was not too rutted, he felt he could get by.

As Jerome's reputation for siring quality foals spread, another problem appeared. Jerome's daughter mares became old enough for breeding. This was contrary to the rule of not crossing bloodlines between sire and daughter. My dad was obliged to recommend another stallion for the mare. This meant that he had to extend the radius from home to other townships and counties. He would have to drive farther, work longer hours, and travel more unfamiliar bad roads.

One day his front wheel hit a rut and he quickly hit the ditch and tipped the truck on its side. He felt panicky when he crawled out of the cab fearing the worst for Jerome. He was relieved to see the horse calmly eating grass in the ditch bank. How that horse jumped out of there my dad did not know.

One thing certain was that Dad had to come up with another way to transport his stallion. Jerome was too valuable a commodity to risk his getting hurt. During the Depression, when dollars were scarce, the $10 stud fees probably earned more in a season than he realized on his farm.

My dad bought a 1929 Dodge coupe. This was a small, dependable car with a short wheelbase, and abundant power to pull a two-wheel trailer. The trailer had to be heavy-duty with truck tires, low reinforced bottom and high sides to transport a big horse. He needed a rugged trailer because he was now traveling into Mille Lacs County to service his stallion. Jerome's granddaughter mares were becoming numerous, and Jerome could not service them, so the radius from home was increasing.

This coupe-trailer combination proved better than the Model T truck, but it still had drawbacks. Jerome proved to be a notorious back seat driver. He was very feisty and aggressive. When he spotted horses in the field along the road he would scream a challenge to any male horses.

Once there was a farmer disking, using a four-horse abreast hitch close to the road. When Jerome spotted them, he issued his challenge scream. He also shifted back and forth in the trailer causing a teeter-totter effect with the two-wheel trailer. The little coupe was securely hitched to the trailer, and the coupe's hind wheels would nearly leave the road. This was before seat belts, and the car occupants would be severely jostled. My dad would lean his head out the window and shout instructions to Jerome. As for a little boy's reaction in the passenger seat, all I could come up with was an enthusiastic, "Let's do it again."

The Dodge coupe still had abundant power and had not been in any accidents, but this pounding by Jerome was wearing it out. My dad had to come up with another way to transport his stallion. He chose a new 1936 Terraplane pickup. My Uncle Bill Nystrom had the dealership for Terraplanes in Foreston.

Terraplanes were developed by the Essex Motor Company and proved to be too far ahead of times to become popular. They were the first to come out with hydraulic brakes, a big improvement, which other auto companies adopted. Some Terraplanes came out with the first steering wheel shifting apparatus. It was about the size of a remote television control that we have nowadays and had a short toggle switch to choose the gear speed. Terraplanes were a luxury car, nice riding, yet very powerful and fast on the road. My Uncle Mearl Miley told me that the first ride he had at over 100 miles per hour was in a Terraplane. Few roads could sustain fast driving, and fewer cars could go that fast.

After installing a trailer hitch on his new pickup, Dad tried pulling the trailer with the stallion. The pickup had a long wheel base, more power, and with the hydraulic brakes, Dad could control the trailer much better. My mother claimed that this new car was too nice to be hauling a stallion around in.

1936 Terraplane

The big drawback with Terraplanes was that in hot weather the engine would suddenly stop. This was called "vapor-lock," and for a long time it seemed to have no solution. Eventually it was learned that the gas line on the engine block would cause vapor lock and would overheat. My dad carried a container of water to pour on the gas line, and this cooled it enough to start. An insulated copper tube was not thought of in the 1930s.

There were no signal lights on vehicles until the late 1940s. Drivers were supposed to signal their turn by rolling down the window and using arm signals. In cold weather some drivers would open their door instead because these cars had no heaters, and this was quicker. The Terraplanes had the door hinges on the rear side of the door, and if one opened the door while moving, it would suck all the way open.

Jerome died of old age in the winter of 1939 at the age of 21. My dad lost an old friend after many years and interesting experiences. He no longer needed a pickup and traded the Terraplane off. When World War II started, all civilian car manufacturing stopped because of the war effort. After the war the Hudson replaced the Terraplane.

High School Champs
by Lloyd Deuel

During World War II, there was gas rationing, 35 m.p.h. speed limit, almost no traffic on the roads, and the armed services had about depleted all available young men who could pass their physicals. The school teachers were nearly all women except for a few older men and a very few men who failed their physical exams.

Farm families were short handed to get their normal work done with their young men off to war, and this resulted in younger kids stepping up and getting the job done. Farm boys especially were expected to do men's work. Town boys were all expected to work too, so we worked on farms, drove trucks, and did construction work. Schoolwork suffered because there was no other choice. High school boys were dropping out of school and joining the services.

In the late summer of 1945, I was working for Harold Luchsinger and Bill Jepp near Foreston helping them fill silos. I had a saddle horse that I used for delivering papers in Foreston, and I would saddle him up and ride the mile out to their farms each morning for the day's work. A notice appeared in the Mille Lacs County Times that there would be football practice for any high school kids interested. I had tried out for the baseball team that spring, and now I would be starting my junior year in school, and I thought I'd give football a try.

I had to hire a kid to deliver my evening papers. I had a choice of paying him 25 cents a day or going cheap and getting an even younger kid for 15 cents a day. The problem was the 15-cent kid was not old enough to read my customer list.

The other problem was that I rode my horse back to town, stabled him, and then had to catch a three-mile ride on Highway 23 to the Milaca High School. It was considered patriotic to pick up hitchhikers, and there was some traffic in the afternoon, but at night after practice there was no traffic. My parents would not allow me to ride my horse to practice. Many times I reverted to the old standby coping mechanism of running two telephone pole lengths and walking one and then running two more, etc. until I reached my destination.

There was one other factor for farm kid athletes. Electricity had only recently been installed on farms because of the war. This meant that after most farm boys walked or ran home from athletic practice, they still had to milk cows by hand because a lot of farm fathers still hadn't installed electric milkers.

When I got home from practice, I had to feed and water my horse and clean out his stall and do this again in the morning. Country boys had to rise early and milk those cows before catching the school bus. We only enjoyed indoor plumbing and hot showers when we were in the high school and after sports practices.

The first afternoon I was late for practice, as were four other guys, and we all had been filling silo. They were farm boys, about six footers, and nearly 50 pounds heavier than I was, and they were farm boy strong and tough. The coach chewed us all out for being late, then pegged the other guys as his starting front four: Jerry Strating, Elmo Norgard, Jerry Talberg, and Jim Halverson.

Our football equipment was pretty well used up. In 1939, the Milaca High School Indians undefeated football team rated "All State" in Minnesota. The school splurged in honor of this team and bought all new equipment for the next year.

After the war broke out, there was no new equipment available to be bought, and we made do with what we had. The helmets and pads were leather, and the pants were heavy canvas. Everything would be stored in crates after the season and unpacked before the next season. A friend of mine told me when I tried my suit on that it usually takes about two weeks before the smell of the guy who wore it last season leaves and your smell takes its place.

I was installed to play center and be linebacker between these four big guys. I loved the tackling on defense, but being a novice, the signals for centering were my undoing.

Every day the five of us would be late for practice because of silo filling. No matter how we tried, we just couldn't make it on time, and the coach would throw tantrums. He was from the North Minneapolis Camden area, where there were no silos to be filled. All he knew about silos was that they were those tall round things sitting beside the big red barns that he saw out of the Greyhound Bus windows on his way to Milaca.

One day he was barking at us when one of the guys interrupted him and asked if it would be better if he asked his dad to explain about why silo filling took so long. The coach calmed down. Fortunately the silo-filling season was about completed. The coach let up on the other four guys, but my bad centering had his undivided attention. It was my defense that kept me on the team.

After two weeks of practice, the coach announced that there would be no practice on Friday afternoon, meaning we could catch the school bus home. When I related this to my dad, he told me that Jake Hoversten wanted me to drive his truck full of little pigs to southern Minnesota, starting early Friday morning. He could see no reason why I couldn't do that for Jake. Jake had learned the rules of the road while driving horses and wagons, and he was a bad truck driver. I had turned 16 years old and had driven trucks quite a bit. We loaded up about 150 little pigs and left Foreston about 5 a.m.

I liked working for Jake. He couldn't drive well, but he was a "chow hound" in that he knew every good restaurant and eating-place between Foreston and the Minnesota-Iowa state line, and we sampled at least five or six each day. We got back to Foreston Saturday evening, and he paid me 50 cents per hour promptly.

On Monday morning at school, a good friend gave me the news that the team had been ordered to suit up to have our pictures taken on Friday afternoon. I was slated to have my picture taken with the first team as center, but I was replaced because I wasn't in school that day. It was good to have friends to keep you posted.

Russ Hill and Dick Isaacson alternated taking my place at center, with Ken Noren and Dave Kuester at ends and Captain Don Carlson, Bob Sjostrom, Jack Dahl, and John Marudas in the backfield. With four big silo fillers up front who wore out the opposing line for three quarters and then came back with even more intensity in the fourth quarter (they were in shape, strong, and farm boy tough), we had a good team.

As for me, I didn't have to worry about signals or centering to the wrong back or flubbing a long snap. I found that I enjoyed playing defense in practice against the first team and the challenge that entailed.

This 1945 Milaca Indian Football Team went on to win the Rum River Conference Championship, and my name was placed on the bottom of the trophy. In the spring of 1946, I made the baseball team starting lineup. Our star pitcher was Ray DeHaan, who was a senior and had pitched for three years. His only defeat in three years came when he was in tenth grade. We were invited to the 1946 State Baseball Tournament in Northfield after the season, but were rained out twice, and then it was canceled. We felt that we would have kept winning until Ray's arm gave out. I have my name on that trophy too.

The next year, when I was a senior, I played baseball again. We collected another Rum River Championship behind the pitching of Ken Noren. This made three trophies with my name on them. I will have to admit that the old saying, "Being in the right place at the right time," would have to apply here.

Lloyd Deuel is a former machinist who lives in Brooklyn Center with his wife Phyllis. They enjoy gardening, woodworking and retirement. A four-time Minnesota Memories contributor, Lloyd has written dozens of stories about his growing-up years in Foreston and Milaca.

My Sonja Henie Doll
by Mary Jo Boots

In 1940, Norway's Sonja Henie was the most popular female figure skater in the world. She had won ten consecutive world figure skating titles and three gold medals in the Olympics. She was often called the Pavlova of the ice for her glamorous demeanor and costumes, and her graceful balletic skating routines that transformed the sport forever. After the 1936 winter Olympics, she turned professional, toured Europe and North America, and starred in ten popular Hollywood films.

My 5-year-old sister Betty and I, a year older, idolized Sonja Henie. We saw some of her movies, and her picture seemed to be everywhere. One fall day we were shopping with Mother in Dayton's department store in downtown Minneapolis, and we begged to visit their toy department. Once there, we made a beeline for the dolls. To our delight, there were several suitcase dolls featured under a big sign that said, "Sonja Henie Dolls."

Sonja Henie fan magazine

Each doll stood proudly inside a blue insert in its large cardboard suitcase, and although each doll was a little different, all were dressed in figure skating outfits like those Sonja Henie wore, complete with ice skates and stockings. More clothes for the doll to change into hung on the other side of the suitcase. The doll I fell in love with also owned a pair of flowered pajamas with a red background, a brightly striped sports outfit with shorts, bra, and beanie, and a white sleeveless party dress with a pleated skirt and blue satin ribbon trim.

After we saw the dolls, we knew just what we wanted for Christmas. There was one big problem though. The price tag said $7, and that was a lot of money for a public school teacher to pay for dolls in 1940-- especially when multiplied by two for two little girls.

For several days we could talk about nothing but the Sonja Henie dolls. Mother and Daddy must have had a consultation, because one day they proposed that we start saving our money for the dolls. They said if we could each save half the cost, we would get the dolls for Christmas. Now we didn't have many sources of income at that age, but we did get a weekly allowance, and we both had birthdays before Christmas. Aunt Lura and Uncle Merle could be counted on for a generous birthday present.

Well, we saved our money in our little tin MJB Coffee banks, and by Christmas we had the required $3.50. We were so excited we could think about little else. We already had baby dolls, but those were the only dolls we owned. The prospect of new dolls was doubly exciting.

The plans were to spend Christmas with our grandma and grandpa in Doland, South Dakota. We watched Daddy load the car with food, presents, and suitcases, and we became quite anxious because we didn't see any package that could possibly hold those big suitcases that held the Sonja Henie dolls. We had our share of the doll money with us, and all the way out to Doland we conferred in whispers in the back seat of the car. Had Mother and Daddy forgotten? Couldn't they afford to pay the balance? Where were our dolls?

Christmas Eve finally came, and Betty and I hung up our stockings on the living room fireplace, the precious $3.50 nestled in the toe of each. Aunt Ruth thought it was terrible that we had to pay for our Christmas presents, but we didn't care. Nothing was too much if we only had our Sonja Henie dolls on Christmas morning. That was still a big worry, and we didn't sleep soundly that night.

Although we were awake in the double bed on the sleeping porch upstairs long before the adults, we knew that we couldn't get up before we were called. Finally the time came, and we went down the stairs--still afraid that there would be no dolls under the tree. I'll never forget the wonderful joy and relief I felt when I saw the Christmas tree with two open suitcases standing underneath. With an ecstatic rush I ran down the rest of the stairs, scooped up my doll and hugged it to me. Betty and I still had a surprise, though. Our dolls were not dressed in their original clothes, but in beautiful black velvet skating dresses lined with pink satin and trimmed with gold sequins. Mother had been busy sewing.

Later that day we went to Uncle Kenneth and Aunt Marguerite's for Christmas dinner, and my cousins Tom and Don pronounced that our dolls had "oomph." Ten-year-old Tom made my doll a fringed western skirt and vest out of ivory colored oilcloth.

For each of the next two Christmases, our suitcase dolls appeared under the Christmas tree wearing new costumes. One year they wore blue satin skating dresses with gold lace and little embroidered flower trims. The next year my doll had a wedding dress made out of a lace curtain. There was a long net veil, perfect panties, bra, and underskirt. Betty's doll had a pink bridesmaid outfit with pink underclothes. We played almost daily with our dolls, sitting on the floor or bed indoors, or on a blanket on the lawn with the suitcases standing up in front of us, and our dolls' wardrobes carefully arranged nearby. Mrs. VanWyck, a neighbor, knit sports clothes for the dolls--ski, tennis and skating outfits, and she purchased wooden skis and poles. I also loved to sew for my doll as I got older, and my suitcase contains many unique costumes.

Yes, as the present tense in that last sentence implies, more than 60 years later I still have the doll and the suitcase. It's a little battered around the edges, but interestingly covered with its original travel stickers. The blue insert is long gone, but packed neatly in labeled boxes is every piece of clothing that came with the doll, and she acquired much throughout many happy hours of play. Every item of her wardrobe is intact, down to the mittens, stockings, extra pair of blue shoes, and skates from her original costume--as well as the oilcloth cowgirl outfit.

At a recent Home Economists in Homemaking meeting, we were asked to bring a special doll and share its history with the group. Of course, I took my precious Sonja Henie doll and told this story. One of those friends suggested that I write it down for _Minnesota Memories_, so that is what I have done.

Mary Jo Boots was an administrator of a program for disabled persons. She and her husband Henry live in Redwood Falls.

Bloomington Civic Theatre's Early Years
by Edgar Simmons

After graduating from Mankato State College, I went back to Minneapolis to look for work and hang out with some of my University of Minnesota friends. I befriended Bill Dovali, who was doing some shows with the Bloomington Civic Theatre.

Bloomington Civic Theatre was started in 1955 by some women who believed the town needed culture to offset the booming suburb's outstanding athletic programs. Their first show was *The Curious Savage.*

For several years their plays, performed at various high schools, attracted audiences and good reviews. After their ground-breaking successful production of *Guys and Dolls* in 1960, however, theatre managers decided to add more musicals and expand their season. Since few other theatres were doing musicals back then, Bloomington attracted top talent.

One night I went with Bill, who was working back stage on their production of *Auntie Mame.* That night I met Gary Schultz, the director, and Gary asked me if I would like to join the group. With my speech and drama minor, I was thrilled to get involved with that theatre.

A few weeks later I found out about auditions for their next show, *Finian's Rainbow.* A mixture of Irish folklore and American social problems, the show's plot concerns a bigoted Southern senator who learns the meaning of brotherhood after magic transforms his skin from white to black. I played the black Senator Ratkin. His transformation took place amidst lots of thunder and lightning. With all the confusion, and with most of the cast onstage, I was backstage dressed exactly like the senator. When the guy playing Senator Ratkin rushed off stage and passed his white hat to me, I replaced him onstage with my black skin. Most of the audience never figured out how the transformation was done.

When I heard that Gary Schultz was thinking of directing Leonard Bernstein's *West Side Story* the next season, my heart skipped a beat. I love that show. I had heard nothing but good things about it when it was playing on Broadway while I was in college, and kids my age knew the music because they listened to the album.

I went to the audition, and Nancy Raddatz, the choreographer, chose me as one of the dancers. I was a Jet named Mouthpiece. *West Side Story* needs solid, skillful dancers. Some of the guys and most of the gals could dance, but others needed work. Nancy took us all out to Bloomington High School's courtyard during the heat of summer and started teaching us slowly. It was hard, but we learned. Step by step she turned us into a cohesive group of dancers. To me, moving your body to music is one of the greatest arts. My favorite number was "Cool," the most graceful dance.

After weeks of practice, we were ready for opening night. I will never forget the butterflies in my stomach when that curtain went up and there I was dancing the "Prologue" with the Jets and the Sharks. The entire show was done with a single set and area lighting. With no scene changes, the continuous action called for careful timing and discipline to provide the necessary psychological breaks between scenes.

Their 1962 season opened with *West Side Story*. That was the same year the movie version of the show won the Oscar as best film. Rumors were flying about that Bloomington Civic Theatre and director Gary Schultz had bit off more than they could chew with the show, but the jam-packed opening performance at Bloomington Senior High School not only quelled doubts that they could swing it but also stood out as a production of breath-taking verve and near-professional style.

Ed Simmons is a retired high school art teacher living in Rio Vista, CA.

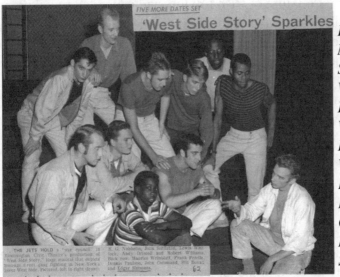

Front Row: K.G Nobbetin, John Surflaten, Lewis Whitlock, Andy Driscoll, Robert Williams Back Row: Maurice Weinblatt, Frank Pendle, Dennis Paulson, John Command, Bill Dovali, Edgar Simmons

A Trip to Jackson and Back
by Donna Doyscher Hawkinson

Dad and Mom were both born and raised in Jackson. All my aunts and uncles on both sides of the family lived there so we would visit them about three times a year on a Sunday afternoon, then drive back home so Dad could be at his barbershop in Hollandale on Monday.

Aunt Ella was probably my favorite. She was older than Dad, and a grandma-like woman. She had a big house with a big porch and swing, a lawn swing, and an upstairs. I loved going there. I remember her front door with its oval glass window, and I remember how she was always there to meet us with big hugs and kisses. It didn't matter if the beds were made or the dusting was done – she made us glad that we had come!

My cousins Dean and Bud were big brothers who often made life miserable for their little sister Marita and me. We both had red hair. I was seven years older than Marita, but we got along well and had loads of fun riding our bikes all over Jackson. We even took the bikes upstairs to visit Aunt Etta and Lois, who lived above the pool hall owned by Grandpa Doyscher and Uncle Harry. Lois was our cousin who spent most of her life in a wheelchair, crippled with arthritis and a multitude of other physical problems. We would bring her bottles of nail polish and talk to her while Aunt Etta worked at the movie theater concession stand.

Marita had roller skates, and there were real sidewalks in Jackson. Hollandale had no sidewalks except right in front of the downtown stores on one side of the street. It was such fun to skate all over town. Jackson had a playground with a merry-go-round, where we spent a lot of time.

I find myself thinking how wonderful it was to be a kid then. I don't ever remember crime, sexual predators, burglaries, or even locked doors! We could go pretty much wherever we wanted to, within reason of course. Aunt Ella and Uncle Leland were always there to bandage our skinned knees and take us up Thomas Hill to the swimming pool. I learned to swim in that pool because Hollandale didn't have one. I usually stayed about a week or two, and then my parents would come to pick me up, or I would take the train or bus back to Albert Lea.

One of those summer vacations taught me a lesson I never forgot. I was about 9 years old, I guess, and was allowed to travel alone after Dad drove me to the depot in Albert Lea and put me on the bus. Aunt Ella met me in Jackson. There were no transfers or layovers, so it was safe at that time. The conductors and bus drivers were kind to little kids traveling alone, and it worked out fine. My parents decided that I would be coming back on a certain agreed-on date.

I had been in Jackson for maybe four or five days, and for some stupid reason, I got really mad at Aunt Ella. Maybe she was sick of having me around. Maybe she wouldn't take us up to the swimming pool when I wanted to go, or maybe she was just too busy to have company. I decided to leave. Without telling her, or without notifying my parents, I walked downtown to the Jackson bus depot, bought a ticket with my last bit of money except for 15 cents that I knew I had to keep in order to call long distance from the Albert Lea depot to Hollandale for Mom and Dad to come and get me.

Donna Doyscher, age 8, young, independent traveler

When I got to Albert Lea, I went into the phone booth at the hotel, called the operator, and told her I wanted to call "2314" in Hollandale. She said, "Please deposit 15 cents."

I hung up, took my little coin purse out and deposited 15 cents. I picked up the phone again, and the operator said, "I'm sorry, I didn't hear the money being deposited."

I panicked! Right away, I knew I shouldn't have hung up when I put my money in, and it was my last 15 cents! What to do? I said, "I DID put the money in. I'm a preacher's daughter, and I wouldn't lie to you. Please, I need to talk to my mother." She must have sensed the urgency in my voice because she let the call go through.

Mom answered, and of course she was surprised that I was in Albert Lea, because I wasn't supposed to be coming home for another few days. She drove in and picked me up at the depot. Of course, she made a phone call to Aunt Ella right away to say I was safely home and would be appropriately punished. And when we got back home, and after Dad came home from work, I GOT IT!! Trouble, with a capital T!

"You don't do this to people who care about you – or anyone else for that matter! Do you have any idea how upset and worried Aunt Ella was when you disappeared?......etc. etc."

I was grounded for a period of time, and I realized what I had done. It never happened again, believe me. I knew I had it coming.

Donna Doyscher Hawkinson grew up in Hollandale and lived in Hoyt Lakes for 23 years. She and her husband Ray moved to Clearwater, Florida in 1980.

Off to War--Three Young Men From Owatonna
by Jeffrey L. Cardinal

Because World War I was the war to end all wars, Americans raised their next generation of sons and daughters with hope that they would escape participating in another great war. This optimism began to fade in the late 1930s, and the bombing of Pearl Harbor on December 7, 1941, dramatically altered family life as citizens made sacrifices in a united effort to defeat two fascist regimes.

Thousands of young people from Minnesota served in the armed services during World War II. From Owatonna, all three sons of Josephine and Al Butsch went off to war, and their experiences affected their destinies. This family was no more special than any other, but they represent the American experience. Three brothers served their country when it was the common thing to do, and while they were gone, a blue three-star service banner hung in their parents' front window.

While becoming part of "The Greatest Generation," all three fought in faraway places and saw things they had never seen before. After marrying into the Butsch family, I found myself asking questions and reading old letters from my father-in-law and his brothers. I talked to two of the brothers and went through letters all three boys sent home 60 years ago. Respect and curiosity drove me to put together pieces of my wife's family history.

They were a typical Minnesota family. Each boy had a wry sense of humor and easygoing manner, and each looked at his circumstances as new, interesting life chapters.

Bob graduated from Springfield High School in 1932 and entered the University of Iowa. In his freshman and sophomore years, R.O.T.C. was mandatory. Juniors had the option to stay in, with a financial incentive of $47 a semester. After four years of R.O.T.C., Bob graduated as a commissioned second lieutenant with no prospect of having to serve in the active Army. He was curator at Arrowhead Museum in Aurora for two years, and then spent two years in Barbados as the Chief Preparator for the Barbados Museum and Historical Society. In 1941 he received his Master's Degree in zoology from the University of Iowa.

Because of his R.O.T.C. training, Bob was put on active call-up as a commissioned second lieutenant later that year when war was declared. He and Miriam Palmer from Newton, Iowa, tied the knot on December 21, 1941, and like many newlyweds of their generation, they started life together in a non-traditional fashion.

Miriam followed Bob to Fort Edwards, Massachusetts for his initial training. He said, "They needed to find a place they could use me so they put me with an engineering and amphibious group." Assigned to the 532nd Engineering Regiment, he continued training at Carabelle, Florida before going to Fort Ord, California, where his regiment completed training before being shipped to the Pacific theater.

During World War II, the Army demanded innovative tactical training with weapons, artillery, air defense and amphibious landings. The concept of combat readiness training was first introduced at Fort Ord. Before Bob shipped out, he thought they were headed for the Aleutian Islands. Miriam knit wool caps that could be used as a liner under his helmet. She said, "All the wives felt domestic," and each made two warm, woolen caps. Bob and his regiment were sent to the balmy South Pacific.

Bob spent time in New Zealand. From there they went to Australia, then up through New Guinea, and on to the Philippines, where he was assigned to Regimental Headquarters of amphibious engineers. A funny incident happened when he was on Mindanao, where General Douglas MacArthur landed on the beach, fulfilling his, "I shall return" pledge to the Filipino people. His arrival was staged and filmed for propaganda purposes, but when MacArthur got off the amphibious craft, he got his feet wet so they had to do it all over again.

When Bob wrote letters home, he would get past Army censors by telling about a type of animal he saw, using his zoological expertise. Those at home could learn his location by looking up information about the animal's natural habitat.

His letters are like a *National Geographic* special. He described exotic birds and a water buffalo that was unique in that part of the world. It is no wonder the censors didn't know what he was talking about. As he put it, "My letters are a dissertation on the natural history of the region."

After dinner one time I pressed him for more about what he did. To my amazement, he opened up and related a few stories. First he said, "When you are shot at the first time, you ask, 'What did I do to him?'" He told of men who were killed because of foolish actions. He told how monotonous the food was. Once he made a fishing lure, and they caught "Wahoo" kingfish to break the routine. Later someone threw a grenade into a tide pool, killing plenty of fish and giving the cooks the pleasure of preparing something new.

I tried to ask more, and for the first time I saw him get angry at my question. Leaning forward towards me, he said, "You could never understand!" I stopped asking because I knew I had hit a nerve.

After Bob came back to Miriam in Iowa City, he felt there wouldn't be many jobs after the war so he decided to go back to school. With help from the G.I. Bill, he earned a doctorate in zoology from the University of Michigan in 1954, and he never left Ann Arbor. He served as director and curator of exhibits at the University of Michigan Exhibit Museum of Natural History until he retired in 1985.

Tom, the youngest brother, graduated from Owatonna High School in 1936 and joined the Minnesota National Guard. He worked for three years at Parrot Hardware before moving to Albert Lea to study business at Albert Lea Junior College, where he met Betty Wayne. When war was declared, he received his call-up for service. This forced him, like many, to change his plans for the future.

The 34th Infantry Division was called to active service and assigned to Camp Claiborne, Louisiana for training. Tom was in an infantry platoon. After field training and maneuvers in Louisiana and Texas, he was selected for Officer's Candidate School at Fort Benning, Georgia. After completion he was commissioned a second lieutenant and assigned to the 350th Infantry Regiment of the 88th Infantry Division at Camp Grunder near Muskogee, Oklahoma. He received more training with the division, moving from one training site to another in the South.

Betty joined him, and they married in Oklahoma, where they made their home until the 88th Division was deployed. In November, 1943, Tom and his division were loaded onto liberty ships in Newport News, heading for North Africa. In 22 days they reached the coast of Casablanca, where Tom saw a French battleship turned over, and his realization of war was profound. He went to Algeria, where he went through intensive mountain training before being shipped to Italy. Tom described Italy, "It was like fighting up one mountain, down another, then across a river, up a mountain, down another, then across another river." He spent most of the war slogging his way through Italy, where it took weeks to go a few feet.

Tom and the 88th Infantry were involved in infamous battles, such as Anzio, Pomerance, Arno River, Po Valley and others. They were the first to arrive in Rome. He told me, "We were instructed not to fire weapons unless someone fired first, to save the historical sites."

When the war ended and Tom was thinking about what he wanted to do, a general convinced him to stay in the Army. For the next 25 years, Tom and Betty, with their son and daughter, traveled throughout the world, never living in one place very long. When the Korean War broke out, Tom was sent to Japan, where he helped establish and train the new modern Japanese army. He retired as a Colonel and lives in San Francisco.

I have been able to get to know Jim, the middle brother, through his letters and by talking to Tom and Bob. Jim graduated from Owatonna High School in 1934 and followed in Bob's footsteps to the University of Iowa. Jim's interest was aviation. While at Iowa, he took flying lessons and got his pilot's license. Like Bob, he had two years of mandatory R.O.T.C. Jim enlisted in The Army Air Corps and was sent to flight school in Corsicana, Texas. When Jim got to Corsicana, he wrote, "The airport is brand new, and we are the first class to be assigned here. We live in barracks that were just finished today, and everything has fresh paint. They just turned the water on tonight." He went on to say they would be flying "Fairchild BT-19-A's--one-wing, open ships."

The first class started with 54 flying cadets, divided into two sections. One flew while the other attended ground school. After four months in flight school, Jim washed out because he was physically disqualified from further flight training.

After his discharge, he came home to reconsider his options in aviation. He stopped at Iowa City's Civil Aviation Authority to see if he could possibly take some courses to qualify as a flight instructor. By December of 1942, Jim was in Burbank, California studying airplane construction at Lockheed. He wrote, "Fletcher aircraft had a contract to train men, at Lockheed's expense, to go to school eight hours a day, and at the end of each day, they paid $2 cash. I went to school five days a week for three weeks." Jim found a room for $3.50 a week near the plant.

Five other fellows lived there, all of whom worked at Lockheed or Vega plants. "We learned how to assemble planes and rivet and drill layout aluminum sheets. There really is not much to it." Jim described California as, "Blackouts, thousand of planes overhead, factories going full blast for the Army... It's all just one big mess of organized confusion..."

Plant work bored him, so he looked for what to do next. Jim considered the Foreign Service with Lockheed, which could pay $500-$600 a month at plants in Africa, Persia, Alaska or the Hawaiian Islands. He tried to enlist in the Army, but his discharge was a hindrance. He submitted enlistment papers again, but this time did not mention the discharge. He was called up and reported to Nashville in December of 1942. Once again he was an air cadet. He felt that all was going well, but at the end of January in 1943, Jim's frustration hit a dead end. He wrote, "Well, the axe fell yesterday. It seems that the Army has been stringing me along. I have been eliminated, and it looks as though I will never fly for he Army again."

But this time the Army did not discharge Jim. They needed all the men they could get, and he was a staff sergeant who could go almost anywhere in the Army. He was looking at taking a five-week course in aerial gunnery, studying maintenance of aircraft, guns and armament, so he could accrue enough time to apply to Officer's Training. Jim didn't like being a "noncom," while Bob and Tom were officers.

Jim opted for gunnery school. Even though it meant a drop in rank to private first class, there was the opportunity to reach the rank of staff sergeant when he finished training, and he saw gunner training as another way to fly. He was sent to Kessler Field, Florida, for school and basic training, which was harder and more tedious than imagined. Through each course, Jim ranked first in his class. After Florida he was sent to Biloxi, Salt Lake City, Denver, Casper, Mt. Hope and Pocatello before he shipped overseas.

While still in Florida, he trained men and put up with heat and sand. He swept sand out of his tent many times in a day, but when he got into bed he had "the beach inside." In Biloxi it was so damp that he could hardly keep his clothes dry. Training was so intense that they had no barracks. Everything was outside so that the men would learn to work on their armaments no matter the situation.

Gunners acquire the ability to take weapons apart and put them back together in any situation, fix turrets, and adjust armaments (bombs). He was learning to shoot .20, .30, and .50 caliber machine guns, the primary guns of the B-24, and he was the top turret gunner in his group.

Jim headed west and met up with his assigned crew and plane. His squadron of B-24s started flying five hours a day, and then their missions went cross country, lasting 24 hours and flying at altitudes of 20,000 feet. Jim saw danger as they trained, and losing men and aircraft to accidents was a fact of life. He didn't seem to give danger much thought.

After a 24-hour mission, Jim unexpectedly got orders to transfer to a new squadron and plane that was getting ready to go overseas. He was specifically asked for, but Jim was furious over his transfer. He wrote, "My old crew will stay here, and now I am with a new crew. They haven't had half the training we had, but I had to be pushed to go."

In February he headed to England via the Southern Ferry Route, arriving February 18, 1944, at their new base at Horsham St. Faith. On his days off, Jim took the train into London to see a few shows. However, within days of arrival, he was flying deep into Germany. Their first mission was March 2, 1944, against Frankfurt.

In a letter Jim said, "I know how ducks feel on the opening day of hunting season. I only hope the Germans don't have any better luck than I had duck hunting." His 458th squadron was involved with D-Day, flying off in complete darkness, loaded with maximum fuel and 5,000 pounds of bombs with the objective of taking out German U-boat pens, gun batteries, and French air fields, hitting coastal defenses in support of the invasion of Normandy, and acting as a diversionary magnet.

Jim wrote, "I wouldn't have missed it for the world. And it's something I will never forget the rest of my life." A month later, on July 7, Jim was listed as missing in action. The telegram came to his mother, Josephine, in Owatonna. At the end of the month she received another telegram listing Jim as killed in action, with no details. Through letters from surviving crew members and the government after the war, the exact details of Jim's death were disclosed.

"On July 7, 1944, while his B-24 was on a combat mission to Lutzhevsurf, Germany, it was hit by flack. While trying to make it to Sweden, they were hit again. Staff Sergeant Butsch was hit by flack when it exploded in the top turret, killing him instantly. Staff Sergeant Gilbert was hit by the same explosion, and five others jumped. While three others were killed and one still in the plane survived the crash, he and the other surviving members of the crew were captured, separated by the Germans, and put into prisoner of war camps."

James A. Butsch died at the age of 28. His body is buried at Netherlands American Cemetery. The grief Jo and Al Butsch felt after losing their middle son was mixed with worry that Tom and Bob were still in some of the war's heaviest combat action.

Thirty men from Steele County were lost during World War II, and many families' lives were changed when their sons went to fight in faraway places. Like many Minnesota families, this particular one was permanently altered. Their oldest son used his G.I. Bill to further his education and achieve his career goal, their youngest son changed his plan of going into business and became a career Army officer, and their middle son was buried thousands of miles away from his Minnesota home.

Bob, Jim, Tom & Al Butsch

Jeffrey L Cardinal was a Michigan freelance writer and author of "Timelines...a Collection of Short Stories". He died in 2004,

Our Big House in Mankato
by Marion L. Forderbrugen

When I think back to my childhood days, as I often do, I feel like I was two little girls in one. For three months each summer, I was a country bumpkin at the lake, enjoying all the things a lake cottage could offer. The other nine months of the year I was busy with things around our house and town of Mankato. Our house at 913 South Front Street, and its large double garage with our playhouse above, held all the fun any kid could ask for. We also had help from our imaginations.

913 Front Street, Mankato

Two girls near my age lived in the next two houses, so along with them and the kids across the street and down the next block, we had lots of playmates. My life was never boring.

The house was a light tan brick with two screened-in porches in front and on the side in back. As you went in the front door, there was a foyer with an open staircase. Off the foyer was the parlor, the dining room with a bedroom off it, and then the kitchen.

Upstairs were four bedrooms and a bath, with a hallway running the full length of the house, ending with a back stairway that went down to the kitchen. Talk about paradise for kids who loved chasing each other-- especially if one of us pestered a sibling or a friend. The chase would start up the front staircase, through the second floor hallway, down the stairs to the kitchen, through the dining room, parlor and back to where we started. If peace hadn't been reached by that time, through all the screaming, the second lap of the chase began.

Our family gathering place was the dining room with its big table where we studied, worked on projects, played cards and read. I was always drawing and painting pictures, and before I could read, Mom read me the funny papers and explained what the characters were doing. We had a radio, and when it was on, we sat looking at it like we do with televisions. I guess our imaginations sent us pictures of what we were hearing. The static got pretty loud at times, but it was worth the noise.

About the only time our parlor was used much was when we had company. At Christmas time it got a workout. Dad built a large square box to hold the tree straight, and inside the box he had a water pail filled with wet sand. It's still the best tree holder I've ever seen. The family got busy trimming the tree with many beautiful glass blown ornaments. I was a fussy tinsel stringer, and I loved putting tinsel on one strand at a time. We would decide which corner of the parlor to put the tree in. I always liked it right next to the foyer because you could see it from all the rooms, and I always felt sad when our tree had to be taken down.

Our kitchen was another gathering place for family and friends. Mom and Dad did lots of entertaining, and our house could handle a gang. There were card games, and Dad often put the large pool table on top of the kitchen table, and the men had loud pool parties there. I loved playing pool, although I had to stand on something so I could shoot the ball.

Mother was a brew master who made home brew and root beer for us kids--and it was good. She had a tall bottle capper that I loved to use, and I thought it was such fun sealing the bottles. The capper went to the lake with us each summer because Mom and Aunt Rose made home brew and root beer there too. We stored it in cases under the beds, and to cool it we put big chunks of ice from the icebox around it.

Like every house, we had a large icebox with a drip pan underneath. On days we needed ice, Mom put the ice card in the front window, turning it to show the number of pounds we needed. The iceman put a big chunk in the street and then started chipping away until it was the right size to fit our icebox. All of us kids waited like bees around honey while he chipped away, and when he finally pulled away, we grabbed all the pieces of ice and sucked on them until our tongues were numb. You'd think it was ice cream.

Dad's print shop, Meixner Printing Company, took up three rooms in the basement. In our dining room we had a bell that we would ring if we wanted to get ahold of my dad or my brother when they were working down there.

Behind our home was a large, two story double garage, more like a barn in size. The full double upstairs was made into a playhouse for us kids, and what a great place that was! Mom and Dad furnished it with lots of old furniture, and we hung our things on the wall. My contribution was all my movie star pictures that I cut out of magazines.

We had no windows up there, but we had a large door, like hay-lofts have, and when we pushed the door open, there was nothing between the ground and us. How we escaped killing ourselves still amazes me. We had the fear of the consequences drilled into us so deeply that we were scared spitless to go within two feet of that big, gaping hole.

The stairway to our castle could be raised and lowered by a rope on a pulley that we worked from upstairs. It came in handy if we saw kids we didn't care for heading for our playhouse. We just pulled the stairs up, and that solved it, but that very action got me in trouble when I called to Richard Pass at the end of our alley and told him to come up. He started running, and I worked like crazy to get those steps up. I was alone and barely had the strength to lift the heavy steps, but I made it just as he ran into the garage and stopped. He started yelling for the steps, and I thought it was so funny because I really didn't like him anyway.

What I didn't know was that Mother was hanging up her washing in the back yard, and she had heard me call to him. He kept yelling louder and louder, so Mother came to see what was going on. She gave me a lesson in etiquette. When you invite someone to come over, you let him or her in. You don't leave them outside yelling at you! Those steps were lowered much quicker than I had raised them.

Each September we had a new girl come to live with us and work for her room and board. She was a student at Mankato Commercial College, and she had the bedroom off the dining room. She helped Mother with housework and watched us kids when our folks went out for the evening. When I look through photo albums from those years, I see many of those girls with our family. When they graduated from the college it was hard to say goodbye to them because they became like older sisters.

We had many adventures in that large brick Victorian home that Mother dearly loved and wanted to live in for the rest of her life. But the Depression came, and then Dad died, leaving Mom with three children aged 16, 14 and 10. She had a terrible load to carry. After a few years of trying to hang on to the print shop and make a go of things, she had the terrible job of disposing of furnishings, keeping only what was needed in the three-room apartment that we moved into on Willard Street, across from Grandma and Grandpa.

We moved out before I grew up, but the years we lived in that great house built up a lifetime of memories for this little girl, and I often think about those days and the fun we shared there.

Marion Forderbrugen lives in Owatonna. She likes to journal, paint water color pictures, raise poodles and create books for her family about her life experiences. She has also written a book of poetry.

The Circus
by Marion L. Forderbrugen

One spring, we girls in our three next-door houses decided to have a circus. We already had three animal acts: Zola's dog Trixie, Gladys Miley's mother's Persian cat (a bad idea), and my cat, Tommy. We were going to have the circus in Zola's yard because there was a vacant lot next door. We figured we needed that much space to handle the crowd we expected to flock in.

We made paper tickets that would sell for a nickel, and it took us about a week to get things organized. After school we practiced our acts and sold tickets. We had to get cardboard boxes and cut holes in them so we could show our cats and dog through the hole (second bad idea). None of our animals had been stuffed into a box before, but that didn't seem to worry us at the time.

The circus day arrived, and we were busy with last-minute details--like getting our pets stuffed into their viewing boxes. I can't imagine today why we thought this was such a great idea because my cat had already been seen and chased by many in our neighborhood as he snatched their birds. But maybe seeing him boxed up would be worth a nickel.

He hated the box, and just when all the kids were getting settled on the ground, Tommy went wild, trying to get out through the viewing hole. He had that box rolling around the yard like a tumbleweed in a windstorm. It was a funny sight; all the kids were laughing and yelling, and they loved it. They thought it was a real act. He was a hit. When I released him, he bolted for home without waiting for a curtain call.

While I struggled to set Tommy free, Zola and Gladys were trying to get Gladys' mother's cat into her box. She was a haughty Persian who loved only Mrs. Miley and had no time for kids. They almost had her boxed when she spotted a tall tree and got a burst of strength.

I never saw a cat climb a tree so fast, and we couldn't get her down with anything we tried. Our little audience of kids had such fun trying to get the second act out of the tree. So far, this circus was a real hit. We hurried with our other little acts because they paled next to the cats'.

Zola's dog, Trixie, was all we had left of our menagerie, and he was lying peacefully on the ground after witnessing the antics of the two cats. He knew he couldn't top them, so we left him alone.

Our circus came to an abrupt halt when we realized Mrs. Miley would be home from work soon. We had a mess to clean up, and her cat was in the top of the tree. When she arrived home, there wasn't a kid or any trace of a circus in sight. We were all inside our houses watching her reaction when she looked straight up at her precious cat in the tree. We never did see the rescue because it was dark when calm settled in next door.

I stayed away from Mileys' house until one day Gladys called me over to see the latest batch of kittens in Mrs. Miley's bottom dresser drawer. No wonder the mother cat was a basket case on circus day. She knew that a circus was no place to have kittens, and the tree was even a worse place!

A circus was never again mentioned in our neighborhood--except when a real one came to town. But I do think the kids got their nickel's worth at ours.

Marion Meixner and Tommy

A Stupid Idea
by Marion Forderbrugen

Mom and Dad were having a party at our house in Mankato, and we kids would be allowed to stay around for awhile to see everyone. Mom had bought me a new pair of black patent leather Mary Jane shoes, and I was going to wear them to the party for the very first time.

I remember getting all dressed up in a pretty dress, new white socks and my new shoes. I looked ready for a party, but one thing bothered me; I wanted to be taller. My mind must have temporarily shut down because I was always taller than most of the boys in my class, and I hated it.

The city was paving Front Street, and the fumes must have seeped into my brain. I went off in search of a stick. When I found one, I used it to put a big glob of the smelly black tar inside the heel of each one of my shoes.

When I put my shoes back on--voila! It worked! I was taller...until the heat of my feet started to melt the tar even more, causing it to come oozing out of the shoes.

I was trapped in more ways than one. I had to take off my shoes before Mom saw me, but it was too late. When I came through the door, Mom stopped me to rush me outside. She thought I had walked in the street, and she didn't want tar tracked in on the carpet. If only it had been that simple.

Poor Mom! When I told her what I had done, she just looked at me in horror. We hurried to the back yard, and I can still see us wrestling those shoes and socks off me so she could get my feet cleaned with turpentine and heaven only knows what else before their company arrived. I was so humiliated.

Those new white socks and Mary Jane shoes never made it to the party, and neither did their owner. I was sent upstairs with my cat to spend the night with my pink feet.

I sat in my bedroom listening to all the fun everyone downstairs was having, and there was lots of laughter--no doubt at my expense--because that episode was just too good for Mom to keep to herself.

To this day, if I see or even smell a freshly tarred street, I'll drive blocks around to get away from it. And I'll always remember those cute, mistreated patent leather Mary Janes I almost wore to a party.

Barney Anderson's illustration of Marion Forderbrugen's story.

Owatonna Scuba Diving Club
by Don Matejcek

It's hard to believe that in Steele County, a place that doesn't have more than about four ponds, one of the oldest, largest, and most active scuba diving clubs in the Midwest is still active more than 40 years after it was established.

When I graduated from Owatonna High School in 1961, I thought I would not have to go into that school again. I was wrong. In the fall of 1961, two self-taught divers offered a scuba diving class as part of the adult education program. John Kroke, a high school teacher, and Jim Dailey, a toy store owner, taught the class for two years. Most class members were law enforcement or rescue workers, but a few of us took up diving as a hobby.

In the spring of 1963, about 10-15 guys formed the Owatonna Diving Club, and all Owatonna scuba diving classes subsequently took place at the diving club. The club was formed to promote diving and to raise money to get a new compressor so we could get air at a decent price without having to drive all the way over to Rochester. We quickly achieved both objectives.

Initially class members received a certificate of completion, but in 1968 we sponsored Marlyn Swearington to get national certification through the Professional Association of Diving Instructors. Marlyn taught diving until 1986, and during those years he gave out about 1800 certificates for different levels of training. In 1986, we paid to have two more instructors, Bill Hildebrant and Leon Ellis, certified by the YMCA. Bill became county sheriff and didn't have much time to teach diving, but Leon taught about 175 students for the next 11 years.

Club membership hit its peak in the 1970s with 130 families. We raised enough money to buy land in downtown Owatonna, where we put up a building. We rent out the upstairs, use the basement for our meeting room, and the garage area for equipment storage. Our members range from divers who do nothing but dive in cold water to some who only dive warm waters down south. Some do both.

We used to go out and find boats, motors, anchors, guns and anything that fishermen or duck hunters lost in the lake. Occasionally we would find cars, and during winter, we would find snowmobiles.

My most memorable diving incident happened the first time I tried ice driving. We have reels now to attach guide ropes, but back in the '60s we attached our ropes to a guy standing on shore. He held the rope tied to the diver like a cowboy with a lasso, and the diver under the ice sent him signals by pulling on the rope. Going under the ice without a guide rope to help get you back out would be treacherous.

I got under the ice my first time and gave a signal tug just as the guy up there accidentally dropped the rope. Feeling a slack line, I figured I'd better turn around and try to get out before I lost my bearings. I swam just as fast as I could, back to where I had just started. As soon as he dropped the rope, the guy who was supposed to be my anchor made a mad dive to the edge of the ice to retrieve it. When the two of us came face to face near the hole in the ice, we were both pretty surprised.

Lately the Owatonna club membership has decreased somewhat because of the condition of our lakes. Over the years the weeds and algae have gotten so bad you can hardly see anything most of the year. Some members have gone up to Lake Superior, and just off the north shore, where shipwreck sites from 100 years ago still interest divers. Both my sons and my two teenage grandsons enjoy diving, and they all learned through the Owatonna club. We still have 90 families in our club, and there are a few teenagers now in classes. They might have to drive far to do any decent driving, but they're still getting good training in Owatonna.

Don Matejcek is a retired fleet maintenance technician for Owatonna Utilities.
The Scuba Club's website is
krypton.mnsu.edu/~dljavens/
dive_htm

Nick McGregor, Don Matejcek get ready to dive the shipwreck America at Michigan's Isle Royale National Park on Lake Superior in 2002.

Gee Whiz
by Michael Finley

My poodle Beau and I are visiting the dog park behind the airport in Minneapolis. It's a huge field owned by the airport commission, and they let dog owners use it as a place where dogs can run free.

My dog is mixing it up with the other dogs. It's a warm summer night, and all the dogs are grinning broadly. I'm stopping to pat a schnauzer on the head, when a big young rottweiler circles round me, lifts a hind leg, and urinates all over my back and pant leg.

Time stops. Several other humans stop and point mutely. One person appears to laugh nervously, but no sound comes out. I look behind me. At first I doubt the dog has hit me -- he must be peeing on the grass behind me.

Then I feel the warmth seeping through my shirt. I feel the looping shape of the stream, like a signature hastily scribbled on my back. To paraphrase the epitaph on Keats' grave: "Here lies one whose name was writ in urine."

My smile freezes and fades. The warm feeling turns cold. The rottweiler gives no sign that what he has done is anything out of the ordinary, or in need of forgiving, and shambles merrily away.

I feel less merry. The collegiality that marked the intra-species gathering only a minute before has dissipated, and I cast about, looking from face to face, seeking to know whose dog did this to me.

Someone informs me the dog's name is Cain, and he is a nice enough dog, about two years old.

I can feel my heartbeat, which informs me I am in a low level of panic. How does one handle a situation like this? Do I get accusatory? Do I demand an apology? Do I falsely laugh it all off, as if it were water off a duck's back? Or do I tuck tail and run home to my agitator and spin cycle?

The owner, a young man who does not look like the type who trains dogs to pee on people, squints at me and realizes something out of the ordinary has occurred. "Your dog just peed all over me," I say dubiously.

"Oh wow," he says. "I'm really sorry." What else could he say?

I get to my feet, stretch and let my soaked shirt flop against me. "I think I'm going to go home and clean up," I say.

People nod like that was probably the most sensible thing to do. Even Beau goes along with the withdrawal, despite it cutting short his evening revelries.

So I'm standing in my basement, plopping my clothes into the washer, with Beau watching from the doorway, and me wondering what I did to bring that on myself, and what lessons I might learn for the future.

And I decide that by kneeling to pat the schnauzer, I had signaled that I was not a person of consequence. A person of no great consequence was of the same order as a lilac bush or a fire hydrant. In a way, by coming down to the dogs' level, I had asked for it.

I decided thenceforward to insist on slightly greater dignity for myself and greater distance between me and the dogs. To be more animated, and less treelike. To speak frequently, and without ambiguity.

And to avoid in future, insofar as possible, the indelible mark of Cain.

St. Paul resident Mike Finley has worked as a newspaperman in Worthington, a TV producer for the University, and a columnist for the St. Paul Pioneer Press. His website is http://mfinley.com

Red Fox
by Michael Finley

I have been walking my dog Beau down along the Mississippi this spring. And this year I have noticed something new. Animals that shouldn't be coming into the city are appearing. Bears in South Saint Paul, coyotes in the western suburbs. And with my own eyes I have seen red foxes on six separate occasions.

This is extraordinary because I have seen exactly two foxes in my life before this -- both times, deep in wilderness areas. The first fox I saw this year was at the Highland Park picnic band shell. He looked at us, we looked at him, and he scampered away. The next time was in the woods at Como Park. The fox bawled -- it is a strange, uncanine sound, somewhere between a goose's warning cry and a calf calling out for its mother. And we saw it -- a small, fine, gray creature, gazing at us with indiscernible intent.

In the 1970s I associated the red fox with my redheaded beauty Rachel. We got this idea partly from the books of Yaqui mysticism charlatan Carlos Castaneda, who detailed the existence of spiritual "allies" that manifest as creatures of nature -- like guardian angels, but you have to be on mescaline to interact with them.

One dusky evening on a hilltop in West Virginia, where Rachel was visiting, a red fox tripped across the road just steps ahead of her, and shot her a look that gave her chills. Somehow, she reported to me, the fox seemed to know everything about her progress in this life, and was coaxing her to hew to the path she was pursuing. So she went to Yale.

Later, spotting a red fox hand puppet at an airport gift shop, I purchased it for her. Sometimes we would have pretend conversations in which I was the fox guide, putting words in the fox's mouth, advising Rachel on what comes next.

The difference between those days and these days is that we were so quick then to "understand" what the fox was trying to say. It was a feral visitor from the nagual or supernatural realm, with a message for us about our destiny. It was our friend, but a fierce friend, who would upbraid us for our failures. Whereas, today, seeing the fox nearly every time I take the dog out, I don't have a clue what it wants. Is the fox by the river male or female? Is it looking at us in hunger or in fear? Is it distressed, or is its appearance in the city a sign of its health?

One thing I know is that I don't want to get close to it, ally or not. Nor do I want Beau tangling with it, whether their DNA is 99% identical or not.

Maybe the fox would kill Beau. Maybe Beau would kill the fox. Or maybe they would play like littermates, but when I got home we would be infested with fleas, ticks, and plague. You don't know.

I do know that, seeing Beau strain on the leash to join the fox, I was witnessing something unnatural -- the meeting of a creature formed by nature, lean and wild, and another who spends each winter night on a warm rug by a full dish.

So I am keeping Beau on the leash. When I walk by Hidden Falls, I expect to see the fox on the forest floor, or perched on a stony parapet. And I expect to hear its crabbed call.

It turns out there is a reason the foxes, bears, and coyotes showed up this spring. We had a warm winter, followed by a cold spring. When the wilderness did not yield quickly to spring, the animals migrated to the city, in search of food.

Little brother, that's everyone's story.

The Taste of Postum
by Graham S. Frear

For me, the truth about mothers lies in a distant memory. My mother, Grace Smiley Frear, died when I was 13, a bad age for a boy, full of unknowns and emotions difficult to understand.

My mother was a university educated woman from a Methodist circuit minister's Ohio family that moved every two years--giving her a certain independence and self-sufficiency. She was of ancient Scottish and English ancestry, coats of arms on both sides. Grahams of Scotland emigrated to Northern Ireland and later to America before the Revolution.

I remember my mother as a slim-waisted, high bosomed woman with erect bearing, rich brown hair in a Gibson girl roll, and a Gainsborough nose. Early in my life, she exposed me to a liberal education that included great music, fine art, literature and poetry. When I was a very small child, my father was working on a Ph.D. at the University of Minnesota. To help financially, my mother took a position as teacher, assistant dean of women, and resident head of the girls' dormitory in a state college in central Michigan. She took me with her.

Mother put me in the care of the Thayer sisters, two maiden women of Appalachian stock who lived in a trim little house near campus and rented basement rooms to college girls. They gave me a secure home full of ginger cookies, fried potatoes for breakfast, geraniums in coffee cans, and home-made bread. My mother insisted I have Postum for breakfast and Ovaltine at bedtime. She had a small dormer bedroom built on the house for me.

I attended the college training school, rich in innovative teaching practices, from kindergarten through fifth grade. I was surrounded by women who cared for me and spoiled me, including many of the 200 girls who resided in the dormitory, women teachers, and friends of my mother. But it was my mother who, though largely absent in my day, dominated and shaped my life. I ate Sunday dinner with her every week in a dining hall full of coeds. During college holidays and long vacations, I stayed in the dormitory, played in its huge basement and trunk room, and prowled its dark, empty corridors with other faculty children.

My mother tucked me in every night, heard my prayers, and taught me to recite the Lord's Prayer, the Beatitudes, the Ten Commandments, the Sermon on the Mount and the Twenty-third Psalm. On Sunday afternoons, we listened to symphonies on the large Philco radio in the dormitory lounge, its green tuning eye still a vivid memory. In her Essex car she took me to movies downtown or in nearby towns, and before I was 7, I had seen the Barrymores and Greta Garbo in *Grand Hotel* three times, and had seen Mary Pickford and George Arliss in *Disraeli,* Richard Dix and Janet Gaynor in *Cimmaron*, and many other great film performances. My education was proceeding in grand style.

My mother gave me books of poetry and brought art books full of great paintings, classical nudes and historic scenes like the rape of the Sabine women and Napoleon surveying the field after the Battle of Austerlitz.

The Thayer sisters saw to my every physical need, my mother to my intellectual and spiritual needs. I was fully aware of how important this woman of grace and intelligence was in my life despite her being largely absent in my daily affairs. I still feel her presence 75 years later.

At Christmas time we met my father half way, in Chicago, at his brother's apartment in Evanston. I recall the elevated trains rattling by, the Christmas tree not our own, and my father and mother talking long into the night after I had gone to bed. My father seemed accidental on those occasions, my mother strongly incidental.

So the power in my life came from a woman I saw only briefly every day or during holidays and summers when we rejoined my father. I recall vividly on weekends in the dormitory my mother often taking me to the empty kitchen in the evening, where we ate bread and butter and lettuce sandwiches with a cold pork chop. What a pleasure and taste I have never forgotten.

After seven years, we returned rather abruptly during Easter vacation to Minnesota and took up residence on my grandfather's farm. I was in fifth grade, abruptly moved from a well-equipped college training school in Michigan to a four-room elementary school west of Minneapolis, across from the farmstead my paternal grandfather had homesteaded in 1872.

As I attempted to adjust to more diverse classmates and fought my way on the playground for acceptance, I sensed a change in my mother, but I was unable to grasp the extent or nature of the change.

My mother seemed to be suffering from some kind of mental disturbance, but I had no idea why. She was finally confined to a treatment facility, and I visited her on weekends. While I played outside, oblivious to what was going on, she and my father talked. I understood very little about what would later be described as a nervous breakdown. We had become settled in Minnesota, at the house where my father had been born. I was so used to not seeing my mother during the week that her absence did not cause any real anxiety.

When she came home after several months of hospitalization, I thought that once again we might be a family, even though I had long since stopped depending on that unity for my survival or well-being. Life went on, as my mother assumed household duties of cooking, cleaning and child care, but as she and my father talked long into the night, Mother seemed more strained and anxious, about what I did not know.

Then one February day when I was out playing with friends in the snow, I heard my father call. When I came into the house I was told, "Your mother is dead." I was more curious than shocked, and while he called the justice of the peace to report her death, I went upstairs to look for her and found her dead in my bed. She had shot herself with a pistol that she had always kept in her car for protection when she and I traveled back to Minnesota in summers. I looked at her with a kind of fascination, not having seen death before. I will never know why she felt she could not go on, but it had something to do with her time in Michigan, my father in Minnesota, the Depression, and me.

My life changed abruptly. Two years later my father remarried--a good Norwegian, Lutheran woman who cared for me, but my mother was gone. And for that matter, my father was gone as well. My roots were cut, and I would live largely by my own devices. My real home did not begin again until I came back to Minnesota from the war and married in 1947. I entered a new, secure phase of my life that produced two fine children and a marriage that lasted 54 years.

I have often wondered what my mother would have thought of me as I matured, went to college, married and had children. I became a teacher as she had been. I loved good music, literature and art. I read and wrote poetry and collected a large library. I have some letters she wrote to my grandmother after she graduated from Wesleyan and moved to Boston. She studied French and traveled in Europe. I can imagine her at the Louvre and the Paris Opera, and I still have her opera glasses.

I also have a bronze art nouveau vase with sterling silver ivy appliqué, inscribed on the bottom, "To Grace from Ben, Boston, 1908. My grandmother told me that Ben was a young doctor Mother met in Boston. I have a bill of sale for two one-carat diamond solitaire rings set in platinum purchased by her in Boston in 1908. My daughter now has those rings. Were they for engagement or investment? She did not meet or marry my father until 1918, when they were both teaching in Colorado.

I wonder about the vase, the diamonds, Ben and the slender-waisted woman who for years heard my prayers and became the most important single force in my life--her presence still strong nearly 70 years later. I cannot look at classical art, hear an opera recording or read a poem by Edna St. Vincent Millay without thinking of her. I still have my first book of poetry, *Silver Pennies*, which she gave me when I was 7. I know she still watches over me. I can still recite the Beatitudes, and when I think of Mother's Day, I don't think of the flowers, sentimental cards, or boxes of candy. I recall with pleasure cold pork chops, arias from *La Boheme*, snatches of Garbo in *Grand Hotel* and my mother's favorite poem:

Grace Smiley Frear

> *I burn my candle at both ends,*
> *It will not last the night.*
> *But oh my foes and ah my friends,*
> *It makes a lovely light.*

I can still taste Postum, although I have had none since Michigan. My mother was as much a state of mind as she was a state of being. She set me firmly on the path I was to follow.

Northfield resident Graham S. Frear is a retired St. Olaf professor of Irish Studies.

Sunday Hanging
by Ken Nelson

Until you have hung upside down in a willow tree with a steel hook around the large tendon in your groin area, unable to touch the ground with your hands, you haven't experienced pain, excitement, and the need to remain absolutely still--all at the same time.

It was on a summer Sunday morning, when we were about 8 or 9 years old, and for some reason we were not at church or Sunday school. In search of perfect slingshot crotches and related whistle branches, my cousin Ray and I had climbed a big six-foot diameter, seven or eight-branch willow tree that grew in our front yard. If the age of the tree crotch was such that it made a good, unbreakable slingshot frame, it followed that the branch extensions above the crotch were the right size and juiciness to make a perfect willow whistle.

Suspended from a strong old branch, high in the upper reaches of this tree, was a steel-link chain, with a nasty hook dangling at its end. When we had harvested a sufficient number of slingshot and whistle material, the race was on to see which of us could get back on the ground first. I chose to slide down the chain, but Ray won the race because I didn't make it all the way to the ground. I was way ahead of him when I reached the bottom of the chain, but as I released my hands to jump clear of the chain column, the steel hook on the end penetrated my brand new pants, tore through the large groin muscle, surrounded my tendon, and suspended me upside down.

Ray disappeared, but either Mom or my sister Viola spotted me hanging in the tree and called Doc Schultz. Mom and Vi raced to my rescue, analyzed my plight, and brought out first the kitchen table and then a tall stool and a hacksaw. They placed the stool on the table, and Vi climbed up on the stool, put me on it, and held me to slacken the chain. As Vi held me as still as possible, Mom sawed the chain in two with the hacksaw.

The dust cloud that arose from old Doc Schultz roaring down Fountain Street at ambulance speed still curls through my mind when I let it hearken back into memory.

The chain sawing operation was completed just as Doc slid to a stop by the table on the front lawn.

Black bag in hand, he jumped from his car, examined me, now lying on the table, and said something like, "We better try and get him in the house." They carried me into the front porch, laid me on a couch, and cut apart and totally ruined my new pair of pants. Without any painkillers, Doc extracted the hook from its grip on my tendon. The memory of severe pain is long gone, but I can still recall the sensation of the swab being swizzled into and through the hole made by the hook.

Where was Ray? They didn't find him until late afternoon--hiding under his bed. He thought I had died.

Ken Nelson and Daisy, taken around the time of the Sunday hanging

Ken Nelson was born in Albert Lea. After a hitch in the Navy, he returned to his hometown and worked at the Midway Machine Shop. He moved to Scottsman Industries, where he worked in engineering, product design, research, and sales. He and his wife Vera have three daughters and six grandchildren. They have encouraged him to write his stories.

Two Tornadoes
by Ken Nelson

The late 1930s provided some very hot and muggy days, but Ben Baarson's grain needed to be threshed. Because of his frugality, it was done by a two-man crew as opposed to a neighborly threshing bee that assembled a dozen teams and wagons that could get the task completed in one day. For several summers, with a sandwich for lunch and usually a warm canteen as a thirst quencher and perhaps a dollar a day, I would be farmed out to Dad's good friend Ben to help his hired man pursue the often rain-plagued event of bringing in the sheaves.

On one of those hottest of days, a thunderstorm developed to the northwest of our midfield straw stack location, and suddenly within the darkening storm cloud, a high level, horizontally rolling tornado formed.

We pulled the pins that attached the eveners to the wagons, and riding those eveners like a surf board, we both headed our teams for the barn. My usually docile team seemed to suddenly sense the urgency of the moment, and instead of allowing themselves to be rein-guided through field and home site driveways, they galloped through the rain ditch, over the road, through the lawn ditch and diagonally across the lawn to the safety of their barn.

Both horses wanted to get into the barn at the same time, and they somehow did squeeze through. But the evener that I had now jumped clear of somehow got stuck in the door and put a stop to any further forward movement. Even more panicked now, the horses began rearing their front ends and banging their heads against the joists of the haymow.

At this extremely exciting, "what do I do now?" moment, the hired man arrived with his somehow less excited team, which I managed to hold while he jumped through the damaged door, moved to the front of my team, and calmed them down. He moved them into the comfort zone of their own stalls, and when the barn dust settled, we both moved back outside to see if we could still see the tornado, since the whirring sound had subsided.

It was still visible, moving northeast toward Clarks Grove. It could best be described as looking like a very large, perhaps 50-foot diameter, dull-finish, galvanized steel culvert, several hundred feet long and rocking fore and aft as it paralleled the long, dark cloud. We never heard of a touchdown in its path so it apparently dissipated in the upper air. Oh for a camera to have recorded it because the undulating moves of its light gray cylinder against the black cloud sky could only be described as awesome.

Ken Nelson and his team in the field

Tornado #2

Small by comparison and qualifying as a very high reaching wind devil, I met this twister between the Hayward corner and David Paulson's place. With my old green John Deere B tractor, I was pulling home a tandem-axel trailer load of firewood from a tree removal site one half mile east of Hayward. In loading the seven foot wide by sixteen foot long by too feet high pile of cut and split lengths, I had, on this dry and dusty afternoon, gazed eastward toward the peat fields of the Petran farm. In the course of the several hours it took to load those sticks, I had observed a couple dozen wind devils form and spin skyward several hundred feet. They were quite black because of the peat soil, and their cyclonic motion demanded mental analysis of the continuing display of an unusual quantity of these phenoms of nature. What was causing so many that relatively still afternoon? Why did they seem to be forming only over Petran's farm? How much of a vacuum did they create to suck the dirt to form that very visible column? What would it feel like to be at the base of one of those columns? Could they actually be powerful enough to cause damage?

Little did I know that the answers to more than half of those mental queries would be made available before I got home. Driving on the shoulder of the road, I glanced to my right and saw a small column developing. The column's forward movement paralleled mine, and its height grew rapidly as we moved along. It turned sharply left, crossed the highway ditch, seemed to pause, and then came straight at me directly over the center of the tractor. It first lifted the battery cover that had two snap hooks plus gravity holding it in place, and then it sucked my hat off my head and a major portion of my breath from my lungs.

I grabbed for the "go" lever, which was also the "whoa" lever of a B Model Johnny Popper and came to a confused stop. I first looked to the rear and upward, expecting to spot my hat spiraling up with the debris that had slapped and stung my face. Nothing--in the moment of confusion, the wind devil was gone--completely gone. But where was my hat? Dismounting the tractor, I walked to the back of the trailer, and there, hidden from tractor-view by the fairly high load of wood, was my hat and the metal battery cover. They were only a few feet apart, and between them was a pair of glasses with one lens broken--my glasses. In the confusion of the moment, I had not missed them.

I have always thought that this particular wind devil met its match, first in the old Johnny Popper, then me, and then the load of wood. When it became overloaded with loot, it gave up, dropped what it had accumulated, and just simply disappeared. In the approximately 30 years since this incident, I could count on one hand the number of wind devils that I've seen. I believe that somehow word got around, and they simply got scared of me.

Vera's Impossible Odds
by Ken Nelson

My wife Vera's brother Bob Jensen and his wife Gloria owned a new condo on the north end of Gull Lake in Brainerd. Their dock was one of a long row on a waterway between Gull and Margaret. We were invited to visit and spend opening day fishing Gull Lake.

On a beautiful mid-May Saturday, we four in Bob's boat trolled amid thousands gathered for the Governor's Opener that was unfolding in the north end of the lake. With no action, and tiring of the crowd, we trolled toward the rock pile near the center of the lake.

Vera, never having developed the feel needed to adjust to a change in speed or depth, dragged bottom long enough to get a strike. When she reeled it in, she had someone else's bait, leader, and line in tow. No other boats seemed upset, so we kept pulling in line. After filling the front of the boat with coils, she pulled in a rod and reel--and it looked brand new.

Using much patience, we lucked out and were able to rewind the entire line back on the reel. With no luck for fishing, we returned home for coffee. As we were tying up at the dock, the neighbor came out of his condo to get something he had left in his boat. Bob asked it they had caught any fish, and his response was, "No, but my granddaughter lost her brand new rod in the middle of the lake, and she's really devastated."

Bob held up Vera's catch and asked the neighbor, "Did it look like this?" As I recall, he was speechless. It was the same rig the little girl had lost in the middle of a very big lake.

What are the odds? Unbelievable. But things do occur in very strange ways.

First Day of School
by Arvin Rolfs

September of 1961 marked the first time, at age 22, that I was actually looking forward to another first day of school without the anxiety and trepidation I had become so accustomed to.

Thirteen years earlier, in 1948, when I was nearly 10 years old and ready to start fourth grade at Kenneth Public School, I contracted polio. Because of the effects of that illness, every first day of school since my release from the Sister Kenny Institute in Minneapolis at age 11 had been a high stress day for me.

Returning to my elementary classes every year was particularly distressing on those first days of school until I grew accustomed to the new routine. Kenneth Grade School was a two-room building with grades five through eight located on the second floor. Because I wasn't able to climb stairs in those years, my father had to carry me up the steps every day for most of my time there. And since the only available restroom facilities consisted of two outhouses behind the schoolhouse, half-days of school were determined appropriate for me: forenoons on Mondays, Wednesdays and Fridays, and afternoons on Tuesdays and Thursdays. Singling out a preteen for special treatment (for any reason) was just as traumatic then as it would be now. The antidote was to just grin and bear it.

My teen years at Luverne High School from 1953 to 1957 were a great improvement-- no special treatment there. But first days of each new school year found me, as always, wishing I could be elsewhere, doing anything else. I always managed to cope with the challenges as they occurred, and even became comfortable with routines as I learned them. But the underlying concern was always with me: Can I do this?

Even after graduation from high school, even after two years at Gillette Children's Hospital in St. Paul for post-polio orthopedic surgery and rehabilitation, even after gaining a more confident outlook on life, those first-day-of-school butterflies followed me, even to Worthington Jr. College.

By day #3, however, those butterflies had reasonably dispersed, only to reappear again briefly on Day #1 of my sophomore year at WJC, shortly after which they again dissipated.

As I prepared for the first day of summer classes at my four-year college of choice, South Dakota State College in Brookings, I felt finally cured of that kid-stuff. I chose SDSC more for its accessibility than its curriculum: flat terrain, reasonably compact campus, about an hour's drive north of Luverne, and ready transportation with my younger brother Dave, who was to begin his freshman year there. I scheduled only two classes that summer to allow ample walking and stop-to-rest time between obligations at Brown Hall, Pugsley Union's food-service, and classes.

That first day of school was indeed unique with no more anxious fretting before the event, and more fretting as I got into the event about whether I was in over my head after all.

What had seemed from the passenger seat of an automobile to be a compact campus was much less so on foot. What had seemed to be ample time was offset by longer than anticipated rest-stops. Sensing the challenge early on, I accepted assistance whenever available. A delivery truck driver offered a ride to the administration building for registration on that very first day, seating me on a milk crate where the passenger seat should have been. "I have to tell you," he said. "I can't be doing this every day, you know."

"No problem," I thought to myself. "I don't plan on registering every day." But I toughed-out the week, regardless.

Mobility was such an issue that the next Saturday at home, I prevailed upon my father to make the hour's drive to Sioux Falls to check out a three-wheeled bicycle I had seen being pedaled about downtown. This was a commercial vehicle with one rear wheel and two wheels in front, supporting an insulated container for peddling ice cream. No, it was not for sale, and no, the operator did not know where such a vehicle might be available for sale. But Dad was able to examine the mechanics of it sufficiently and determine that he would talk to Leonard Rogness, the blacksmith in Kenneth, on Monday about the possibility of building one like it, without the icebox.

The next Friday afternoon as Mom and Dad arrived at the dorm to take me home for the weekend, Dad was all smiles. Yes, he had talked with Leonard Rogness, but Leonard was skeptical about how suitable the machine would be. He would have to weld two bicycle frames together to make one, and he was concerned it might be too cumbersome for me to handle. But, while still considering it, Dad had found a better deal.

Fey Brothers in nearby Edgerton had a motor scooter dealership, and Dad discovered a three-wheeled electric golf cart that they were sell-ing cheap. It was cheap because golf carts were not in big demand in southwest Minnesota in those days and, cheaper yet, because they had bought it at an estate sale and didn't get registration papers, which meant I probably couldn't get license plates for it either.

This was a double disappointment. I was looking forward to using a self-propelled vehicle for my personal development. I would have pre-ferred a three-wheeled, gasoline powered motor scooter for greater range and speed (like a Cushman), envisioning even commuting on my own between home and college on weekends, or whatever other ways it would contribute to a greater sense of independence.

Even referable to a Cushman would have been a vehicle I had seen advertised in *Popular Mechanics* magazine-- the King Midget, a Jeep-like vehicle with an aluminum body (the older ones were of plywood), chain-driven, powered with a Wisconsin engine and having an enclosed cab with Plexiglass windows, which my scooter sadly lacked.

But whatever my wish-list then, the scooter proved to be the per-fect solution for getting from point A to point B on campus in a speedy and safe fashion, and it was ultra reliable, even in sub-zero and snowy winter. It was geared for street travel with a maximum speed about 20 m.p.h., and its four six-volt batteries provided a week's worth of running about. The dormitory manager permitted unlimited access to the dorm's external electrical outlet for re-charging, but an over-night charge once a week was sufficient. This was truly a dream arrangement!

Because of its functionality and dependability, I not only survived the summer session, I triumphed over Freshmen Week! In spite of the ignominy of a registered junior having to partake in freshman activities, I did so, and still kept my respect. On fall registration day, I scheduled classes back-to-back, so confident was I of the scooter's prowess.

So confident was I that I even arranged to give a ride to Murray Doeden, a friend and former WJC classmate from Lakefield, now a junior in the school of pharmacy, to show him my new wheels.

By prior arrangement I hustled over to Scobey Hall right after lunch to pick up Murray, show off my scooter, and give him a ride to his first afternoon class in a building adjacent to where my next class was.

Scobey Hall was separated from the rest of the campus by Medary Avenue, heavily traveled South Dakota State Highway #77. As Murray and I sailed down Medary, I made a quick left turn into the campus to beat the traffic, and I felt the side of the scooter lift. "Whoa, that'll give Murray a thrill," I thought momentarily. But it lifted even further, and then everything capsized, pitching Murray, books, and me onto the street with the scooter sliding on its side.

As Murray was helping me to my feet, he noticed his books lying in a pool of battery acid. As he dropped me to retrieve his books, I landed in that same pool. After righting the scooter, he helped me up a second time, but as I got the scooter going again and offered to continue the ride, Murray said, "I think I'd rather walk."

Not willing to miss my first day of Spanish class, I walked into class as unobtrusively as possible, left pants leg drenched with battery acid, abrasions on my left elbow and both knees, hair disheveled. But I survived the hour and decided to go to my final class for the day, chemistry, and after that, to the student dispensary to get patched up.

Back in the dorm room, as I bent over to untie my shoes, I remember thinking, "Boy, these synthetic fabrics must be acid resistant," and then my pants leg fell apart. That was the first of three pairs of pants I managed to ruin: that one, plus the pair already in my laundry bag that got contaminated as I tossed the distressed pair on top of it, and the pair I put on next to drive the scooter to a service station to get it decontaminated.

While at the station, I noticed the scooter's headlight was lit even though the switch was off. In checking that situation, I turned on the power switch and accidentally nudged the throttle lever. The scooter jumped into reverse, and as I grabbed for the arm of the rearview mirror, hoping to check its progress, it dragged me to the ground and slammed itself into a car parked at one of the pumps. The only damage to the car was a slight dent in the chrome strip along the rocker panel. Although it was an older model car, the owner claimed it was in pristine condition. He felt $10 would probably cover his cost of repair.

I made an SOS call to my brother Dave to bring his car with a spare battery in the trunk. He got to the station after the incident was resolved, saving me the embarrassment of having to explain the whole mess to him. I do believe I told him later about the collision at the gas pump, but I know I never did tell Dad. Even so, Dave was still more than a little miffed that already on the first day of classes I had to use the emergency backup battery that Dad had stashed in his trunk of the car.

College life settled down for me after that. But it was gratifying to know that I could deal with mishaps and still survive. And I did manage to graduate from SDSC some 42 years ago. But my first day there remains my most memorable and most encouraging first day of school, ever!

My dream car, King Midget, Model 1960.

Arvin Rolfs grew up in Rock County, survived polio, taught English, German and Spanish in Bird Island and worked as a systems Analyst at Agribank in St. Paul. He and his wife live in Brooklyn Center.

My real dream-machine, a reality check

Doc Hanson
by Neil Palmer Kittlesen

When I was about 4 or 5 years old, I had a problem with constipation. My parents took me to see Doc Hanson in Frost. He examined me and told them that I would grow out of it. They felt he didn't take it seriously and took me to a doctor in Bricelyn, whose diagnosis was that there was nothing he or anyone could do and that I would die.

Not accepting that, Dad responded that they would take me to the Mayo Clinic for another opinion. The doctor replied that I was "a nice boy and worth saving." I think my dad felt angry that this doctor would think there would be any child not worth saving. The doctors at the Mayo Clinic gave me a very thorough exam, and I still remember the enemas! They concluded that Doc Hanson was right and that the problem was, in fact, one that I would grow out of, and I did. My parents always trusted Doc Hanson after that.

We frequently played games in the vacant lot between the bank and the post office. One day when I was 10 or 12 years old, while we were playing baseball, I got hit in the eye with a bat. I was the catcher and was crouched too close to the plate. Bill Isakson was the batter, and he brought his bat back sharply to get ready for the next pitch. The bat struck me in the eye, and I thought it drove my eyeball into the back of my head.

Bill grabbed my hand, and we went off to find Doc, who was just two doors away in the hardware store. He looked at my eye and told me that I would be all right. I asked if there would be any lasting effects and he replied, "Well, I'll tell you one thing; you'll get a hell of a shiner!" I did, and that was the only ill effect besides a lot of pain.

Doc loved playing pool, and when a limping guy came looking for him at the pool hall, Doc asked what was wrong. "I think I broke my ankle," the guy said.

"When did it happen?" Doc asked.

"Day before yesterday," was the reply.

"Well, if you could wait until now to come see me, you can wait a little while longer while I finish this game," Doc said, and everyone was satisfied.

My niece, Karen Nesheim Parker, recalls getting a shot for her bronchitis in the middle of Main Street. Doc was driving off on an emergency when they flagged him down. "What do you need?" he asked through his open car window. When he learned that her bronchitis was flaring up again, he told her to roll up her sleeve. He opened his bag, got the medicine she needed, opened his car door, and gave her a shot of penicillin right there in the middle of Main Street and sped off to take care of the emergency.

Karen remembers another time when she was sick in the middle of a blizzard. Doc asked Karen's mother, my sister Dorothy, what he could bring along for a treat. Karen loved Albert Lea grape pop. Doc got the pop and persuaded a farmer to take him to Rake on his tractor with the front loader because that was the only way he could be sure of getting there in the storm. He gave Karen the medication she needed, the pop she wanted, and he stayed at her bedside all night to be sure she would be all right.

When my dad was 70 years old, he had serious stomach pains after every meal. Doc examined him and was pretty sure it was cancer.

Dad went to the hospital in Albert Lea for an x-ray. The report came back negative. Doc sent Dad back for another x-ray, and again the report was negative. This time Doc got in his car immediately and drove 30 miles to Albert Lea to see the x-ray for himself. "There it is, right there," he said as he examined the x-ray.

Doc operated on Dad a few days later. After the operation, Doc showed Dad's stomach to my brother John and me. I still remember seeing Dad's entire stomach lying in a white enamel tray. Doc picked it up, sliced it open and showed us the huge cancerous growth that surely would have taken Dad's life very soon. Dad adjusted to life without a stomach quite well and had eight more good years, living to see his youngest daughter Helen graduate from St. Olaf College.

Kristin Bromeland Juliar posted this story on the Frost web site recently: "When I was 11, in 1965, I dislocated my little finger the Sunday that the Twins were playing in the World Series. My mom drove me to Doc's house. He came out to the car, grumbling about being interrupted during the ball game, popped my finger back into place and told us to go tape it up. You just don't get healthcare like that anymore!"

Doc had everyone's medical chart in his head, and usually it included about three or more generations. His charges were always very low, and he never mailed a bill to anyone. My son-in-law, John Wentz, recalls Doc making house calls for his family in Blue Earth. When his dad asked Doc, "How much do I owe you?" Doc replied, "How about five dollars; does that sound about right?" He believed that people would pay him when and if they could. If they paid a little at a time or never at all, he accepted that as the way things were.

Doc died in 1994. At the funeral, Larry Anderson delivered a tribute on behalf of all of us who knew and loved Doc. Larry gave me a copy of what he said to be included here:

"When the city of Frost recalls its first century, it is likely that no name will be more fondly remembered than that of Dr. Lewis Hanson. Perhaps no one will ever again touch so many lives in this community. Devoted to his family and his community, Doc truly became a legend in his own time. All the stories about Doc have one common thread. They are all stories about a country doctor, a brilliant man of compassion who tended to the needs of his neighbors nearly all the years of his life.

"Doc claimed to have delivered more than 3,000 babies – 'Not bad,' he would boast, 'in a town of 300 people.' We remember the school vaccination programs where Doc would give shots to the entire student body in a matter of minutes. Often before we could get our hands out of our pockets or our sleeves rolled up. We remember his instant emergency procedures during football games, when Doc would rush in from the sidelines and pop joints back into place so fast that injured athletes didn't miss a play.

"We remember Doc seeing more than 100 patients a day, some receiving treatment right in the waiting room to speed things along. Doc was always on duty. If you saw him in the post office and asked him to look at your throat, he would oblige. If you were sick at night you either went to his house or called him to make a house call. He always responded. He provided affordable access to rural medical service that politicians today will never understand or be able to duplicate. Doc was the end of an era.

"He was one of the first to see a need for an area nursing home, and he became a primary promoter of the development of St. Luke's Lutheran Home. Doc was concerned that the Frost area would need an ambulance after he retired. For years he had provided a sort of ambulance service by transporting patients in his car – often at speeds that scared people back to health. But he knew that the community must make plans to get along without him. He helped make things better by working with other leaders to develop a local volunteer ambulance service that continues to serve the area today. He served for years as chairman of the school board. He was a member and leader of his church. He donated land for what is now known as Hanson Park.

"Doc treated patients from Frost and Bricelyn and Rake and Kiester and most every other town within 50 miles. He was a wonderful physician because he knew us. He knew us not only as patients, he knew us as people, he knew us as neighbors, he knew us as family and friends."

This is an excerpt from pages 76-81 of Neil Palmer Kittlesen's book, "Growing up in Frost," copyright 2000, Kirk House Publishers. Mr. Kittlesen lives in Mendota Heights

Whizzers
by Steve Swanson

Everyone wanted wheels after the war. Between 1941 and 1945, non-essential travel was restricted and tires and gasoline rationed. No one drove anywhere. In 1946, the travel-starved endured endless waiting lists to buy new tires and the first post war cars. Gas was plentiful again.

For us kids, the earliest peace-time pathway to mobility was the Whizzer motorbike. Named, strangely enough, for Supreme Court Justice and former University of Colorado running back Byron "Whizzer" White, and advertised in magazines by movie stars like Alan Ladd, the little bike motor was the cheapest thing in motorized transportation, and it was readily available.

A Whizzer motorbike is now considered collectible, and fully restored it brings up to $5000. But back then the kit was shipped from Pontiac, Michigan to your front door for an affordable $65. No license or insurance was required. I paid for my Whizzer with one month's work on the St. Olaf lawn crew at 40 cents an hour.

The three-horsepower Whizzer engine mounted easily on any full-sized boy's bike, although Schwinn Roadmasters and Black Phantoms with springs on the front fork were preferred. The engine clamped inside the frame triangle, a tear-drop gas tank mounted on the bar above it and power got to the back wheel via a pressed tin belt pulley stove-bolted to the spokes.

To get a Whizzer going, you opened a compression release, pedaled the bike, and let out the clutch. To stop, you back-pedaled like on an ordinary bike. You could help the engine climb up the steepest hills by pedaling, adding human power to engine power.

The amazing little motor vehicle could hit 40 miles per hour and would go 125 miles on one 20-cent gallon of gas. Our awkward and labor-intensive one-speed bikes suddenly had the range, speed and versatility now enjoyed by multi-speed mountain bikes.

We went everywhere–Faribault, Cannon Falls, Farmington, and even Minneapolis. We zipped all over town, especially favoring the now-closed road that rolled and wheeled around Carleton Lake in the upper Arboretum. We drove maintenance staff people at both colleges crazy by constantly pretending we were motorcycle racers and zooming around and around the football field on the quarter-mile cinder running track.

After two carefree summers, our Whizzer motorbikes were rendered obsolete by the appearance of girls in our lives. Two on a Whizzer was precarious and painfully unromantic. Our hormones drove us to motorcycles and cars.

Steve Swanson is an author, St. Olaf English professor, and Lutheran Minister in Northfield.

King of the Ring
by Steve Swanson

I chatted with Johnny Dudley recently and recalled with him a mid-century shared memory of a summer carnival attraction in Northfield.

During those years, right in the center of the whole carnival with freak show tents, games, and food booths encircling it, was a boxing ring platform. Standing in it, night after night, was a scary, heavyweight-looking guy with a two-day stubble that added to the effect.

The barker/referee challenged any farm boy or tough city slicker in the crowd to step into the ring. If anyone could last three minutes with the big bruiser, he'd win $25.

On the night Johnny Dudley and I were there, a long silence followed the challenge. Guys nudged each other like little Mikey's brothers in the Life cereal commercial.

"You try it."

"Not me, you try it."

No one moved--especially me. Then Johnny Dudley stepped forward, climbed the stairs, and stepped over the rope and into the ring. There was a hush in the crowd. Many of them knew Johnny.

As the referee put gloves on him, I grew worried. Johnny was much smaller and lighter than the carnival champion. "He'll get killed," I thought. Johnny slouched to the center of the ring, hands at his sides, looking like he had never been in a boxing ring before.

When the gong sounded, Johnny's gloves came up from his sides like lightning. POW, POW, POW! The big, scary guy was on his backside in ten seconds. He sat there shaking his head from side to side, his eyes glazed. He put his gloves on the mat, partly to steady himself and partly to push himself if he had to. It was apparent he didn't want to.

The referee called the match, claimed some sort of foul, and wasn't going to pay...until he looked out into the hometown crowd and saw that Johnny's friends had begun to look unruly, maybe something like a lynch mob.

He paid. The crowd cheered. Johnny told me that much the same thing happened to him in Faribault later that summer at the Rice County Fair. There not only was a $25 prize for staying in the ring, but a $50 prize if any hometown boy could knock out the carnival champion.

Johnny knocked him out cold. The referee refused to pay, however, claiming the champion had hit the referee's knee going down, and according to the Marquis of Queensbury rules and carnie justice, there had been no knockout.

Johnny Dudley never got his $50, but no one could take away his real prizes. He won several Minnesota and Iowa Golden Gloves Boxing Championships as a middleweight between 1946 and 1951. After that, he fought professionally as a light heavyweight in preliminary events in Des Moines, Duluth, and other towns under the name Jack Murphy. Although he was undefeated in twelve matches, he was forced to retire from the ring at age 23 after he lost some fingers in a farming accident.

John, who continued to farm near Northfield, still likes to reminisce about his fighting career. But he's most proud of his family, whom he describes as a gorgeous wife and five wonderful kids. He likes to joke, "They all can beat me up now." He has an easy-going, friendly way with people, and his conversation is peppered with genuine interest and concern for his family and friends. Guys like John Dudley constantly remind me that the very toughest of men are often the most quiet and gentle.

Under Control At All Times
by Carol Keech Malzahn

After we celebrated our daughter's second birthday on February 9, 1981, we started planning for our second child. By the end of March, I suspected I was pregnant. By the middle of May, the doctor confirmed it and set my due date for December 28. Christmas came, and everyone was nervous that I would go into labor, but we made it to all the holiday gatherings without incident. December 28 came and went with no baby.

I drove to Mankato each week for appointments at the Mankato Clinic. The doctor said he would see me in the hospital any day now, but I'd better make my appointment for the next week just in case. I listened to him say that for four more weeks. By now people had stopped calling me to see how I was doing. I figured I was never having that baby.

On Wednesday, January 27, I was driving home to Minnesota Lake from my weekly appointment, big as a house and quite disappointed that the doctor hadn't kept me and done a C-section. I was wondering how the heck I was going to face another week in this condition. When I drove around the curve on state highway 22 and started down the big LeSueur hill just past the Terrace View Golf Course, I could see a red Hermel candy truck in the ditch at the bottom of the hill, facing the river. We had a record amount of snow that winter, and the ditches were full.

I thought maybe I'd better pay more attention to my driving and started slowing down. As I proceeded, I saw another car sitting in the other ditch and thought maybe the roads were really icy, and I'd better go even slower. I was completely around the curve, coming safely to the bottom of the hill. In full view facing me, on the opposite side of the road, sat a Highway Patrol car. The sight of it made me hit my brakes. It was just a natural reaction, wasn't it? The rear end of my car started to fishtail.

My husband's words came to mind. He said, when we purchased our front wheel drive Toronado, "You can't go in the ditch with this car because it has front wheel drive." I was either going to end up in the ditch like those other two vehicles, or I was going to smack directly into that Highway Patrol car. It all happened so fast! I'm not sure exactly what I did, but I obviously did it wrong, and I did go into the ditch.

I remember the car spinning around at least once, probably twice. I heard the swish of snow. Pop bottles in the back seat all went crashing together with the rest of the groceries I had purchased before my doctor's appointment. I was flung across the front seat. We wore no seatbelts then. Of course, it wouldn't have fit across my pregnant belly anyway. Then THUD…my car came to an abrupt halt. I had not heard the sound of metal crashing, so I figured I had missed the Highway Patrol car.

I carefully sat up and peeked through the windshield to see where I had ended up. I was facing the opposite way in the opposite ditch, and it looked like I was heading back to Mankato. When I looked in my rearview mirror, I could see the Highway Patrol car parked directly behind me, maybe six car lengths away. Thank God I had missed crashing into him! I was brought up to highly respect and fear the law, so I was definitely afraid of Highway Patrolmen.

The snow had kept my car from going too far into the ditch. I was thankful I had missed the bridge, the river bank, or any oncoming traffic, but I was freaking out about "the law" sitting behind me. I had spun a cookie right in front of him. Was he thinking I had done that on purpose?

As he got out of his car and walked to mine, I could see passengers in the other ditched cars watching him. I wondered if I should fake going into labor and try to freak him out as much as I was freaking out. I certainly was pregnant. I thought he would probably call an ambulance. There would be paramedics. I sure didn't want to pay all those expenses, and I actually felt fine. It was the first time in the past four weeks I was happy to feel that little foot kick me from the inside, practically taking my breath away. We were both okay physically. Mentally was another story.

My car was still running, and I pressed the button for the electric window. I looked up at Mr. Highway Patrolman. The sun was glinting off something on his hat so I could hardly see his face. He said, "You picked a fine place to park."

I could hardly believe my ears. He had a sense of humor at a time like this? I was wearing a huge winter coat so he must not have even noticed I was ten months pregnant. I thought maybe I should tell him.

He looked over the inside of my car and said, "Just stay where you are, ma'am. I've got a tow truck coming to pull out these other ya-hoos. I'm sure they will be happy to add one more to their list as long as they are going to be here anyway." He turned and walked away! Whew! I was relieved beyond words. All I had to do was sit and wait for the tow truck. No speech, no ticket, no injury, no damage done.

A couple of minutes went past, and here came a sanding truck down the big hill. Great! Too little, too late. A couple more vehicles passed through the slippery valley successfully and continued on their way up the other side of the hill. I sure wished I were one of them.

A few minutes passed with no traffic. Then a lady driving a full-sized, tan four-door, with kids jumping around in the back seat, came down the hill. My eyes fixed on her. Something was not right. She was sitting up very straight and tall. As she passed beside my car I could see her mouth was gaping open. She could have fit her fist in it! Both her hands were glued to the very top of her steering wheel, and the rear of her ve-hicle was fishtailing just like mine had done. I turned as far as I could to watch, and then resorted to looking in my rear view mirror. Her car spun around once, twice, then three quarters of the way around, on her third spin…. BOOM, CRASH, BANG…. The rear end of her passenger's side made swift contact with the front driver's side of….I could not believe my eyes. Yes, she smacked directly into the Highway Patrol car! She had done exactly what I was so deathly afraid of doing! Unbelievable.

As I was chuckling at how extremely fortunate I was and what bad luck she and that patrolman were having, here came her car, with bumper hanging and a huge dent in the back fender, rolling past me like she was just going to forget this ever happened and head back into Mankato! The kids were no longer jumping around. She finally came to her senses and pulled over in front of me. As I sat between her smashed car and the smashed Highway Patrol car, I could see it was not a good situation.

Once again, in terror, I watched in my rear view mirror as the Highway Patrolman got out of his vehicle, straightened his hat and walked to the front of his car. He bent over, checked out the broken headlight and dent, started shaking his head, and headed toward our cars. I wanted to shout as he strode past, "Look who picked a fine place to park now!"

I sighed in relief. As he walked on towards her smashed vehicle, I could see him reaching into his back pocket to pull out his ticket book. He spent several more minutes visiting with this woman than he had with me. I could see her hands flying through the air as she spoke. He stood there writing on his ticket book. She put her head down on the steering wheel as if she were weeping. I could practically hear the rrrrrip of that ticket as he stuck that piece of paper through her window. I felt her anguish.

It was a bright, sunny, very cold January afternoon. I'm sure Mr. Patrolman was not very comfortable, but I had not thought about his comfort. He had impressed me as being smug and arrogant during our brief chat. I could tell by his demeanor his ego was damaged along with his patrol car. Where was that tow truck?

Oh man, he turned and started coming back towards me. His arm gave me the "roll down your window" motion. He bent down and poked his head in my window. "Ma'am, I'm afraid I'm going to have to give you a ticket. You crossed the center line. If you want to contest it, be in court on February 3. Otherwise, send your fee to the address shown on the bottom of this ticket." RRRRRIP….. "Here you are. Have a nice day."

I was too flabbergasted to say anything. I closed the window and started to examine my ticket. My husband was not going to be impressed. How were we going to pay for a tow truck and now a traffic violation ticket? It was my first ticket. I had never before so much as spoken to a Highway Patrolman! I was definitely stressing to the max.

It seemed like an eternity, but the tow truck finally showed up. They pulled me out first because they said I was the easiest to reach. The others were going to have to be winched out. I could stay in my car.

"When you get home, you'll want to have your husband get all that snow out from underneath your vehicle," the man said as he handed me the bill. I wrote out a check for $45. He said he gave me a group discount and departed, chuckling.

At 7:30 a.m. on February 3, the day I was supposed to appear in court, I gave birth to an 8 pound, 2 oz. healthy baby boy, Paul Leslie. He didn't appear to have been affected by the car accident.

My husband called the clerk of court to reschedule my court date. I remember whispering about it so the nurses wouldn't think I was a criminal or something. Men, wouldn't you know? He rescheduled my court appearance for Friday, February 5. We rescheduled at least twice.

My day in court finally came. I was petrified. I wore my favorite camel colored, corduroy blazer and matching turtleneck with forest green, polyester flared pants. I thought I looked as good as any lactating mother of two could possibly look under these stressful circumstances.

The bailiff stood in front of about 20 of us and rattled off how we were to behave and what we were supposed to do. It all sort of ran together in my mind. All I could remember hearing was if we were chewing gum, we were to dispose of it before we spoke in front of the judge. In order to speak to the judge, we first had to plead guilty of our offense, and then the judge would hear our story. At NO time were we supposed to approach the bench unless the judge requested it, and then we were not to touch any part of the judge's desk. Do not speak until the judge asks you to speak. The bailiff spoke so fast my mind could not absorb it. I was frightened. Then I heard, "All rise" for the honorable judge somebody presiding over the district or county or precinct or something very distinguished and official sounding.

We had to sit and wait for our turn. I felt like a criminal. It was very interesting listening to everyone else's stories. I was counting my blessings that I was not in their shoes. What was I doing here? Why didn't I just pay the fine? I was actually hoping to be last so I would not have an audience.

One man just could NOT bring himself to plead guilty to his offense. He would plead innocent and then start rattling off his story in his own defense. The judge slammed down his gavel and repeated his question. "How do you plead-- innocent or guilty to your crime?"

The man would reply, "I didn't do it, and I'm not saying I did. I'm innocent!" The bailiff had to remove him from the courtroom. I decided I was guilty of crossing the center line after all. Let me out of here. I was too scared to move.

Finally I was called to stand in front of the judge. The bailiff yelled my name and reason for being there. "MALZAHN – CROSSING THE CENTER LINE TRAFFIC VIOLATION." My knees were shaking, my hands sweating, and I figured I would never be able to breast-feed my newborn another day. The judge asked, "How do you plead?"

I started out with a shaky voice, "Guilty," I managed to squeak.

The judge said, "Approach the bench. I cannot hear you."

I slowly approached the bench, being ever so careful not to touch anything! It felt a little better to be closer to the judge. He was older, like my father's age. I felt like I could just talk to him without everyone else having to hear me. The judge was paging through my report. When I stopped and looked up at him he said, "You have rescheduled this court date since February 3."

"Yes, I was in the hospital giving birth to our second child."

The judge started rubbing his forehead and shaking his head. My heart dropped. I thought he was upset with me for wasting his precious time. "Proceed ma'am. What happened the day you crossed the center line?"

I got to the part where the patrolman told me I picked a fine place to park, and the judge started to rub his forehead again. I managed to continue without hyperventilating.

The judge stopped me. "Did the patrolman give you a ticket then?"

"No," I explained.

"Did the patrolman ask if you were all right"?

"I can't remember, but maybe he did"

"When did the patrolman present you with your ticket?"

I said, "Not until after another lady spun around on the ice and crashed her car into his."

Now the judge was looking up at me. He glanced at the bailiff. I got the feeling they had heard this story before. The judge sat and listened patiently to the rest of my story. The entire time he was rubbing his forehead and shaking his head. It was very difficult to choke it all out.

When I stopped he said, "Are you finished?" I nodded, feeling as though I had failed terribly and should have stayed home with my two little children.

"Is the arresting officer present for this case?" the judge asked and stretched his neck to look around the courtroom.

I almost gasped. Had I exaggerated or embellished my story, and was I going to have to defend myself to this officer and his side of the story? Whew! There was no response.

Finally the judge pronounced my sentence. Glaring deep into my soul he said, "You will be placed on probation for one year, meaning you will not have to pay this fine unless you are ticketed again for any other reason within the next year. I hope you realize how extremely fortunate you and your baby are. And always remember this – no matter what the road conditions are, you are still responsible for having your vehicle under control at all times." His gavel slammed down.

I did not get arrested or ticketed within that next year nor have I ever spoken to another Highway Patrolman since that infamous day.

Paul Leslie graduated from Maple River High School and joined the United States Marine Corp. He is a military policeman.

Carol Keech Malzahn was raised in Sveadahl. Now a Minnesota Lake resident, she and her husband Art enjoy small town life and all it has or doesn't have to offer. They are soon to be grandparents for the second time.

Mud Babies
by Alice Steilow

It was a beautiful day, the sun was shining, and big white clouds floated overhead like fluffy sheep in the pasture. We'd had a long, long summer with no rain, and the heat was almost unbearable. Every day seemed to be hotter, but this day was about 90 in the shade. What a great day for us kids to go out and play.

My sisters, Dolores and Francie and I were tired of hot days. Longing for rain, we went over to the side of the house and laid down in the little grass remaining in the shade. There we were, the three of us, lying in a row with our hands cradled under our heads, watching white fluffy clouds change shapes, and we tried to make out what they looked like. One reminded us of a large tree in our grove. Another looked like a dog with a pig on its back, and then there was the sheep without any legs, and a turtle with a long tail. Francie thought she could see a man in one of the clouds, but as hard as we looked, Dolores and I could not make out the man she saw, but then she didn't see the house on wheels that we saw.

When we had spent a couple hours just resting in the grass watching the clouds, one started to turn gray and then another and another. Soon the clouds started to churn and turn darker, and some were very dark with shades of green mixed in. "Rain, rain--do you think we might get some?" we wondered.

We heard a car coming up the drive. Dolores jumped up to see who was coming, and it was our aunts, Clara, Agnes, and Ruthie, and our uncles, Walter and Wilmer. Oh boy, now we could play all afternoon while they visited. Of course, we had to go in and say hello and give them a little of our chitchat. While we were in the house, the day seemed to get darker. Soon lightning flashed and thunder boomed, and three little girls put their hands over their ears and got closer to Mother or one of the aunts, just in case we got too afraid of the boomers.

As rain came down, Mother jumped up to close windows and mop up water that splashed through the open door. The rain came down so hard that we couldn't see very far. Daddy said he wished it had rained a couple of weeks ago so his crops would have been better, but he was really happy to have what he called a million-dollar rain. At least he would have hay to put up for the cattle and horses.

We stood by the window and watched until rain only came down in a soft pitter-patter, then asked Mother if we could go out and play in the mud. It had been a long time since rain, and Mother and Daddy were busy visiting with the company. Somehow Mother must not have been listening very well because she said we could go out if we took off our clothes and went out in our panties. That we did…and boy did we pay for getting muddy. But it was fun.

We went out in the driveway where there had been about 6 inches of dust in the car tracks. Now you must understand that there was no gravel or anything on the road as most roads were dirt back then. First we floated stick boats down the muddy stream that led toward the ditch. That was fun for awhile, but it got kinda old so we crawled into the mud, and soon we were rolling and splashing muddy water at each other. That was fun so we crawled through the mud to the ditch where the water had collected. It was only about a foot deep so we played there for awhile, then crawled up to the house and called Mother. That was something we shouldn't have done because when she came to the door and saw her three "mud babies," she let out a yell and sent us to the shed where the shower was located.

The shower consisted of a 50-gallon barrel on the southwest side of a shed roof. Daddy carried water from the well and climbed the ladder to fill the barrel. He had fixed a pipe into the barrel and into the shed. There was no shower head or anything, just a pipe that you adjusted the flow by a turn-off handle, and I was much too small to reach the shut off.

Mother was really mad at us for getting so muddy, hair and all. All she did was point to the shed, and we knew what was coming--a darn good shower.

Now, I was the smallest so she was there to see I got all the mud off. Dolores and Francie fared a little better, as they were able to get clean themselves. I believe to this day Mother took all her fury out on me, because she held me by the hair under that damn pipe with water pounding down on my head. She scrubbed and scrubbed to get me clean, and to this day, I hate water, and I think about that experience every time I wash my hair under the shower.

Three clean little naked girls ran for the house with their towels flapping in the breeze. We couldn't help but laugh as we dressed. I don't think Mother was too happy, but our aunts thought it was a hoot. I guess Mother finally got over her shock of seeing us standing by that door as black as black could be, but I will never forget that shower.

Now, many years later when some of the grand kids come, I let them play in mud puddles, but they have to do their first wash up under the hose in the yard. After they get the gobs of mud off and their feet clean, they can come in and have a nice warm shower without someone holding them by the hair. I really don't think Mother had a choice but to get me clean, but I swear I almost drowned that day. We've laughed about it through the years, and now she is gone, and I know she was doing it with love…Miss you, Mom.

Alice's family--the Nilson kids--all cleaned up and older than in this story. Standing: Betty (age 7), Alice (age 11), Dolores (age 14), Francie (age 12), Billy (age 6), Sitting: Sonja (age 1) and David (age 4).

Daddy's April Fool's Joke
by Alice Steilow

The day started out as a beautiful sunny morning, and the mud was ankle deep as three of my sisters and one brother and I started out for school. We knew there would be mud if we crossed the field, so we stuck to the road and walked two miles instead of one mile across the field. We were really putting on our thinking caps because what kid didn't like to get muddy? But we remembered that anyone who brought any mud into our one-room school had to get the broom and clean it up without leaving so much as a piece of dust.

After reaching the school and trying to catch some of the kids with an April Fool's joke, we set out to do our class work. It wasn't long before the teacher let out a little squeal as she sat down on her chair that one of the 8th grade boys had put a tack on. Someone in the back of the room with a little disguised voice said, "April fool."

Now that wasn't too funny to her so she picked up her ruler and walked down each aisle of desks asking every child if he or she had put the tack on her chair. All the little kids were afraid she would blame them, but I am sure she knew who the culprit was because when she came to Richard's desk she slammed the ruler down on the desk and said, "Did you do it?"

He couldn't deny it because her actions took him by surprise. He just admitted his folly and took the punishment that was coming to him. In a loud voice so everyone could hear she said, "Richard, you will write a 1000-word theme and have it in by tomorrow, and if it is not done you will stay in at recess and after school for one week, and you will write your theme on why you thought it would be so funny to put that tack on my chair."

Richard wasn't amused, but he said nothing and only hung his head while she went on to give him a good tongue lashing and handed him a piece of paper to start writing on, and again said, "Your theme will be on putting tacks on other people's chairs. Do you understand that?"

The rest of us had a hard time to keep from laughing out loud, but we knew we didn't dare. After that incident, we all kind of lost our fun thoughts about doing any April fool's jokes on anyone for awhile. At recess time my little brother hollered, "Gopher," and pointed in the direction he pretended to see it. Everyone started in the direction that the so-called gopher was seen. One of the boys ran inside to grab a pail of water to drown it out, and when he came running back with the water, my little brother hollered, "April fool!" We all had a good laugh about that. Even Richard couldn't keep the smile off his face.

The day seemed to last forever. It was so nice outside we all wanted to be out instead of having to sit there inside that old stuffy one-room school with 30 students. Any kind of a game would be more fun than that. Finally it was time for the last bell to ring so we found our dinner buckets (mostly old syrup pails) and started out for home. The last thing we heard as we headed out the door was, "Richard, don't forget your homework."

The afternoon was so nice with the sun shining down and making shadows on the ground. We ran and tried to step on each other's shadows, calling it the shadow game. I don't know who came up with the idea, but it was fun to see who could do it without falling down or running into the person you were trying to shadow.

Looking up at the huge white clouds billowing overhead made us really get in the mood of spring and long for the time we could spend outside without having to put on loads of clothes to keep warm. We forgot about the mud we had to put up with until it dried and made our long driveway passable.

There was a car coming down the road behind us, and it slowed and stopped. It was Daddy coming home from town. He said we'd better ride home with him because the driveway was pretty muddy, and maybe it would be covered with water. We all piled in with him and thought the ride was pretty good because we would have longer to play when we got home. My sister Betty told Daddy about the tack on the teacher's chair, and then we all laughed out loud, something we hadn't dared to do at school.

In only a matter of minutes we were at our driveway. Now the driveway had very little gravel on it back then, so the tires started to spin in the mud. There was a hill, and down at the bottom of the hill we could see water standing across the road. It wasn't very deep, but Daddy said he probably would get stuck so he would walk home and get the horses to pull the car across.

He left us with the idea he would be back in a short time and told us to just wait. There we sat and waited, and waited, and waited. With five kids in the car, the bickering started, and then everyone got more impatient by the minute. We sat and we sat and we sat, thinking that any minute Daddy would be coming for us. Then we decided he had to start chores or something like that.

The beautiful white billowing clouds had long ago disappeared from overhead, and in their place darkness was creeping in. Finally we decided we had to brave the water and walk home. We grabbed our things and started down the hill. I think Daddy must have been watching to see when we got out of the car because he came part way and hollered, " April fool!"

Daddy was not one to pull practical jokes on us kids, so we had thought nothing of doing exactly as we were instructed. He told us to wait, and he would go home and get the team of horses to pull the car through the mud.

How humiliating it was for a family of kids who thought we could pull the best April fool's joke on someone else to be caught unaware. We tramped into the house hoping there would be some good food on the table as we sure were hungry as bears. Mother met us just as we were coming in and said, "Keep the mud outside, and then come in and wash up." She didn't have to say that a second time because we were really hungry after waiting so long for what turned out to be an April fool's joke on us.

Alice Steilow and her husband Richard have lived on the same farm near Clinton for 57 years. They have five daughters, one son, 22 grandchildren and 31 great grandhildren. Over the years they have had nearly 100 foster children. Alice worked with handicapped people for 31 years.

You Lost Your Mitten, You Naughty Kitten
by Kaye McMasters Klukow

Walking four long blocks to elementary school was a cold, bone-chilling trek on winter days when a strong north wind blew across Eastside Lake in Austin. I wore wool slacks under my school dress, a hat, muffler and woolen mittens. Sometimes I walked with my new friend Susan Woodfill, who lived along the route. Sometimes she was not finished with breakfast when I stopped to pick her up at her house a block from mine so I would continue on my way, and Susan would run and catch up with me.

On one particularly cold day, my mother offered to let me wear her warmest leather mittens with sheepskin backs. Although they were large and loose, they were so much warmer than my knit mittens. I wore them mindful that they were Mother's precious belongings that she entrusted to me.

As I walked alone, wearing Mother's mittens, I crossed Highway 16 at the closest corner instead of going to the distant corner where a crossing guard kept watch for children. The bridge over the dam was always interesting, so I slowed my pace as I ran my hand along the railing, knocking snow into the creek below.

Suddenly Susan caught up with me from behind, grabbed me and hollered to scare me. It really worked. I jumped and jerked my arms, and in the process knocked a mitten off my hand. As it disappeared into the creek below, I began to wail. Oh, I knew I was in trouble because I had not guarded Mother's mittens with my life.

Susan was apologetic, but I was not to be comforted. I looked over the railing for a long time but could not see anything that looked like a mitten. Finally, realizing I might be late for school--another unforgivable sin--I slowly trudged off in that direction. All I could think about was how I was ever going to be able to tell Mother that I had lost her mitten.

As I hung up my winter clothes in the cloakroom, I wondered what I should do with one mitten. Should I leave it at school, and maybe Mother wouldn't realize I had worn her mittens today?

School started with the pledge to the flag, and as we sat down. Susan came into the room, very red-faced and smiling. How could she smile on a day like this? Didn't she care about what had happened? It really was her fault, if you got right down to it. Every time I looked at her she smiled. Was she making fun of me? By recess time, I was contemplating avoiding her, but she ran up to me with so much enthusiasm.

"Hurry up and get your coat on. I have a surprise for you." Susan was beside herself with excitement. Before I had my coat buttoned, she was pulling my arm and heading for the playground. "Over here, in the snow pile," she coaxed. I was bewildered because I didn't see anything. "Dig in the snow. Look what I found for you."

With my mittenless hands I dug away some snow and discovered my mother's mitten. "Where did you get this?" I was starting to catch some of Susan's enthusiasm. "Is it really mine?" I asked.

"I climbed down the spillway, and I could see the mitten on some rocks in the creek," she explained. "It never even landed in the water."

But how did she ever get it? Susan was a daredevil, but I could not imagine her crawling out on the dam and stepping from rock to rock in the freezing creek. "It was easy," she bragged. "I wasn't scared at all."

"Thank you, thank you, thank you," was all I could say. I was going to be eternally grateful. When I returned to our classroom, I looked at the two mittens at the same time so I knew I was in possession of both.

What a wonderful gift my new friend had given me! We became good friends for four years, until she moved to Brownsdale. She taught me some of her daredevil ways, but I didn't put many into practice. Usually they involved breaking a rule or two, and that was not something I did very well or very often. I don't know why Susan buried the mitten in the playground snowbank that day. Maybe she wanted to surprise me. The important thing was that my mother got her sheepskin mittens back, and I don't remember wearing them again.

Conger resident Kaye Klukow worked as a technical writer for Streater Industries. She has three adult children and nine grandchildren.

Booby Trap
by Jesse Reisdorph

Evelyn and Horace Carson, my sister and brother-in-law, were proud of their home in Morgan and kept it in good repair. They were concerned, therefore, when it was repeatedly vandalized. Their aluminum door had a solid panel on the bottom, and someone had been kicking it in. After fixing it several times, Horace was getting ticked off. He and Evelyn had an idea who the culprit was, but they didn't have enough evidence to approach him or his parents.

Horace pondered ways to get the evidence he needed. Finally it dawned on him. Why not set a booby trap, a tactic he had learned from his stint in the Army during World War II. Although the Army had used hand grenades, concussion grenades, trip wires and cameras, Horace decided to rig a simple camera.

He decided to take the family to a Sunday evening movie. I think they went to the second show because it would have been too light earlier to conceal the camera and the wire that tripped its use.

They set the booby trap and went to the show. Not really expecting results on their first try, they were surprised and elated when they got home and found that it had been sprung. They could hardly wait for the film to be developed.

In the meantime, the suspect was telling neighbor kids that Horace had shot at him. Of course, it was the flash bulb that made him think that.

The kid must have been pretty cool because he came over to talk to Horace. Horace mentioned the cap he was wearing and complimented him on it. The boy was flattered and said, "No one here has one like it because I got it on a trip this summer."

Then Horace said, "That's funny. I have a picture of a boy wearing a cap just like that." The boy knew immediately that the jig was up and that Horace held the cards. He begged Horace not to tell his parents. Horace dropped a hint that he was thinking of calling the police, and the begging began in earnest.

The police advised Horace to let them handle the problem as that might discourage the boy from committing more acts of vandalism and getting into more trouble. Horace let them do their job.

Several years later, in 1988, Horace had a stroke that left him without the use of his right arm and leg. One day, this very same young man, dressed in a suit and tie, called on Horace to thank him for what he had done for him. He wanted to show Mr. Carson that he had grown up to be a real man.

Jesse Reisdorph was an industrial arts teacher in Morgan for 25 years, starting in 1952. Now retired, he enjoys writing. He and his wife Lenora have two adult daughters and five grandchildren.

My Dad's Hired Hand
by Anne Troska

Some of my favorite childhood memories involve my dad and helping him with farm work. Dad was a great lover of horses, and for many years he kept a team, even though he did the majority of his field-work with a tractor.

Jack and Dewey were a couple of gray geldings. Jack was calm; Dewey didn't like things sneaking up on him. Dad liked to use his horses to make hay. Of course, he had to have hay to feed the horses. I think it was something like vertical integration. He said he needed them to make hay and haul manure, but of course the tractor would have served just as well.

There is just something about the communion of a man and his horses that can't be matched with a machine. I used to love to go into the barn at milking time on a cold winter day. I can still hear the hollow sound of the feeding horses as they nibbled with their velvety soft lips and great teeth in the wooden oats box, and the stomping of their huge feet in the straw bedding.

I can feel the steamy warmth of the cattle, in from the snow to the safety of the barn, and the slow chug of the milker as warm milk gushed into the pail. All the cats sat at attention, hoping for wasted drops of precious milk, and every once in a while, as he finished stripping out a cow, Dad would squirt a warm stream at them as a reward for their patience. I used to think that the barn wasn't really such a bad place for the Baby Jesus to be born. I'm sure all the animals welcomed him, in their innocent tolerance, more lovingly than much of the rest of the world.

When I was very small, Dad used to put me on Jack's back while he led him to the water tank for a drink before leading him to the barn for a well-deserved rest. Jack's dappled gray coat was warm and scratchy under my bare legs as I sat on my lofty perch. And when he dipped his head to drink, I felt a thrill of danger, as though I might slide off the world, right over his head.

On hot summer days, I used to wait at the bottom of the hill in the alfalfa field to catch a ride with Dad driving home a full load of loose hay. I can still feel the lazy sway of the wagon as I lay flat on my back in the fragrant alfalfa, watching the peaceful clouds drift over a summer blue sky. The creak of the heavily loaded wagon blended with the slow "clop, clop" of the team's huge feet and the jingle of their harness. I knew I was safe, because my dad was in charge. My love of my dad is always blended in my mind with the smell of horses. Life was sweet, but times were changing. I eventually became old enough to help with farm work.

I live on the same farm I grew up on. Being an only child, and a girl at that, I got stuck with lots of jobs I was not fond of. Perhaps I should say that Dad got stuck with me. At any rate, when I was 11 years old, Dad decided I was old enough to take charge of the team while he stacked the loose hay coming up from the hay loader. "Just keep them in a straight line, and don't let old Dewey see that machine coming at him from the rear," my father instructed.

Proud to be entrusted with such an important job, I held tight to those reins with a grip of iron. We plodded down the field in an orderly fashion, and then it was time to turn around for the return trip. "Take her nice and wide," my father instructed, and I thought I was doing famously, until Dewey got a glimpse of that infernal machine out of the corner of his eye. He bolted, dragging the faithful Jack along with him.

Dad, who was trying to get through a load of loose hay from the rear of the wagon, was hollering, "Whoa! Whoa you #*# horse!" Meanwhile, my grip of iron pretty much disintegrated to terrified hanging on. We were heading toward the downside of a steep hill, with a creek waiting at the bottom. I sure didn't want to end up there, upside down under a load of hay. Dad finally got hold of the reins, and soon he had the team quieted down, but that was the end of my day as a team handler.

Another great job was driving the tractor while my father rode the binder to cut oats. The oats field was on the same hill where I had my adventure with the horses. It was pretty steep, and I was driving an old narrow-wheeled Farmall across the side hill. Dad said he didn't think it would tip over, but just in case, I was supposed to be ready to jump. Now there was a statement guaranteed to give me peace of mind!

The oats field was prime territory for bumblebee nests, and I was deathly afraid of them. They loved to buzz around the tractor's exhaust pipe and also around my head. Once I just got off and ran for home, leaving my angry father swearing out in the field. We had a nice chat about that later!

Dad really did not have an easy lot with me as his hired hand. I was also in charge of driving the tractor to pull the loads up into the hayloft. I was supposed to listen for him to holler "Trip!" and then stop. Well, the tractor was pretty noisy, and I probably wasn't paying quite enough attention, because the next thing I knew, Dad was running behind me madder than a hornet yelling, "Stop! Are you trying to pull it through the end of the barn?"

I announced that if he was going to yell at me, I wasn't going to work for him anymore. Unfortunately, work stoppage was not an option, and I had to clean my ears out for the rest of the day. If only I had been a good substitute boy. But I was not. I would rather read a book, and I would have read one on the tractor if he had allowed it.

Funny how time changes my view of things. I would give anything now just to have him holler 'Trip!' for me, just one more time.

Anne Jenson Troska is the proud mother of five and grandmother of thirteen. She lives on a farm near Alden and, weather permitting, can usually be found in the garden with her hands in the dirt.

Pigs in the Woods
by Anne Troska

Once upon a time, I literally lived in the "little house in the big woods." When I was 3 years old, we moved to a farm near Clarks Grove. Our farm was known as the Hunsey farm, but had been leased by members of my father's family long enough to also be known as Jenson brothers' farm.

Surrounding the area were acres of oak woods made almost inaccessible by the rapier sharp thorns of thousands of gooseberry bushes. Living across the road from us were Albert, a Norwegian bachelor in his 80s, and his unmarried sister, Turina, who was over 90. Albert was something of a recluse, and was rarely seen out and about, but for occasional trips to town for supplies. Miss Turina liked to interact with the community when she could, and would walk to the nearby country school for gatherings.

The couple discouraged visitors, and their privacy was well maintained by a couple of quite unpleasant dogs that patrolled the property. To make things even more interesting, Albert had about the meanest old jackass you ever saw. He was a mangy gray beast, with walrus-like yellow teeth and flying feet that he used as lethal weapons. But even worse than that, he could let loose with a bray that put bagpipers to shame!

All of this piqued the curiosity of the neighbors, and conversations at most gatherings eventually got around to the goings-on, or lack thereof, at the strange household across the road. Our farm was just up the hill from the country school I attended. The school was surrounded on three sides by Albert's woods and ponds, and we had several wooded acres across the road.

Albert was a great believer in letting nature take its course. He used to raise pigs in the woods; or rather the pigs raised themselves. He never fed or housed them that I know of. The sows foraged for acorns and anything else they could find, and had their litters in the shelter of those prickly gooseberry bushes.

The boar pig was likewise wild and free, and one sure way to make folks scatter was to holler, "Here comes Albert's boar pig!" He also had the occasional Holstein bull wandering around. All of this combined to make life an adventure at recess time.

The schoolyard was separated from the woods by a barbwire fence, and we were all warned to stay well away from the woods, but what is that to a kid, except a challenge?

I clearly recall a little foray of my own when I was 6 or 7 years old. The springtime woods were in full bloom, with tempting clusters of dog-tooth violets and dainty yellow buttercups. Being a resourceful child, I thought I would just go in and pick a bouquet for the teacher. I successfully climbed over the fence and was helping myself in a lovely little glen of flowers when a loud "Woof!" came from the other side of those darned gooseberry bushes.

There, in maternal splendor, lay a huge old sow and her pride-and-joy piglets. Tossing posies to the winds, I raced and stumbled back to the barbwire fence as fast as my chubby little legs would carry me, only to hook my skirt on the barbs. At this point, tearing my dress was the least of my worries, and I let it rip as I made my terrified way to the safety of the school. I didn't know how lucky I was.

Later, one of Albert's sows got my father cornered in his own barn, and Dad had to take refuge in the manger where he whacked her repeatedly over the head with a 2 by 4. Dad said it didn't even make a dent in that mean old she-pig's head, and he was saved by the excited barking of our faithful dog, Smokie, who drew away the pig's attention until Dad could make a break for it. I learned plenty of lessons in that one-room school house, not the least of which was staying on my own side of the fence!

A Man's Best Friend
by Mary Kalkes James

I came home from Northfield High School one day in the '30s and found my father lying on the couch in the kitchen. He was moaning with pain, and my mother looked very concerned. Our bull had attacked Dad. It was early winter, and we'd had ice storms at our farm in Dundas on the West Cannon City Road. The stock tank in the barnyard had flowed over and then, to make maters worse, it had frozen solid. The entire area was a sheet of ice. My father had been trying to thaw out the pipe that carried water to the tank when our normally docile red polled bull became enraged and attacked him

The bull knocked my father down on the ice, and Dad could not struggle to his feet to escape from the cow yard. The bull was about to trample him when he caught the ring in the bull's nose. Our faithful Towser, a shepherd heeler, went for the bull. This distracted him briefly, but he returned to his attack on Dad. Again Dad grabbed the bull's ring and called to Towser. The dog attacked furiously, whereupon the bull turned his attention to the dog and bunted him on his back. Dad said that the dog howled in pain, but when he heard Dad call again, he returned to the fight.

As my father was rolling toward the fence, the bull attacked him again, and my father grabbed the bull's nose ring again and was jerked up and down on the ice until Towser's bites caused the bull to once again turn his attack toward the dog. This went on much too long, but finally my father managed to reach the fence and roll under to safety.

Dad told us over and over, "Towser never left me; he saved my life. Even when he was injured, he kept coming back when I called him." My father didn't go to the doctor, even though my mother and I urged him to. He had several broken ribs and was severely bruised. He said, "I don't think the doctor can help me, and anyway, we can't afford to pay him."

Dad had a stiff shoulder the rest of his life, and Towser limped for a long time. Dad died at age 93, many years after Towser died of old age.

Mary Kalkes James taught at six country schools in Rice County. She lives in Northfield and winters in Florida, and she has four children.

Finding Character in a Little Town That Time Forgot
by Judith Hambleton

I arrived in Minnesota Lake on January 1, 1994, still quizzical about why I came. The town was not unlike Lake Wobegon, "the little town that time forgot," that mythical town made famous by Minnesota's own Garrison Keillor. As a professional interim minister, I had traveled to places as far north as Canada, as far west as Billings, Montana, and throughout the Twin Cities. Now here I was in southern Minnesota, about 30 miles from the Iowa border. The town of about 750 people offered fewer amenities than any place I'd been.

It was while I was making my first house call on a cold January day shortly after my arrival that I discovered something about why I had come. It also influenced an important decision I later made, one of the most important of my life.

I ventured out into the countryside on that cold January day to make my first visitation. The cold tundra of rural Minnesota can be quite deceiving to the newcomer, taking on the appearance of a smooth table top blown white with snow and wind. Little did I know that beneath the snow on both sides of the roadway sometimes lay very deep ditches.

Few things daunted me in my role as an "in-between" pastor-- an interim female pastor. An elderly gentleman told me at my first assignment that he thought no woman should be preaching in his church and that I should not expect to see him in the congregation while I was there. Little did he know that behind his words was one of the reasons I was called to professional interim ministry. I intended to introduce women in the pulpit to as many churches as possible.

On another assignment, right before worship began, a young man strode up to me as I was arranging items in the chancel area. His manner was threatening, and so were his words. "You don't belong here! You're a woman!" Seeing my predicament, some ushers quickly escorted him toward the back of the church. When the congregation filed out at the end of the service, my distress ebbed entirely as two small girls gazed up at me admiringly, and I received a few positive comments such as, "Isn't it nice to have a woman in the pulpit for a change?"

So with a stiff upper lip and out-thrust chin I ventured out into "Minnesota cold" that fateful January day. A town or city has street signs to guide a stranger on her way. The countryside has landmarks. Having been told which landmarks to watch for, I was confident I would find my destination easily. After fruitless efforts, however, I knew I needed help and headed for a house I saw in the distance.

As I timidly approached it and knocked on the door, I heard barking coming from behind the house and soon saw bounding around the corner a huge black dog baring his teeth menacingly at me. I scurried to my car and quickly shut the door, my heart pounding loudly in my ears.

By this time it was dusk, and the wind was whipping snow into circles in the road ahead of me. I decided it was futile to continue my search. Town was about six miles behind me, I guessed. I could easily turn my compact car around right where I was. I had done the very same thing many times in Minneapolis successfully.

As I was completing my turn, however, the front of my car lurched downward. "Oh, no!" I cried. I was stuck for sure, and only the sudden arrival of spring or a John Deere tractor could release me. Assessing my situation, I decided to walk to town, silently counting my blessings that I had chosen my warmest winter coat to wear that day. Not wanting to be entombed in this frozen tundra, I scrambled out of my car and started walking.

As I headed toward town, I noticed a black dot on the horizon off in the distance. I thought it might be a car, but since it was so far away, I quickly dismissed the possibility that someone had seen me. Then the dot started to appear larger. "They're coming my way!" I exclaimed.

As the car approached, I could see its occupants: a round faced woman on the passenger's side and a clean-shaven man at the wheel. Both were peering at me intensely. It turned out they drove out of their way just to be sure I was a woman. And if I was, they knew I would need help. Driving back to their home, they got a tractor, returned, and pulled my car out easily. As they waved me on my way, I breathed a sigh of relief as I watched them disappear into the darkness.

That was my introduction to Minnesota Lake and the character of its people. I found the town and its people so appealing that when my assignment at the church was completed two years later, I purchased a piece of property where I built my dream home – a log home. Eventually I opened it as The Gathering Place on Pelican Pond, a bed and breakfast that also had been a dream of mine. I moved to Arizona in 2003, but I have warm memories of that little town that time forgot.

Minnesota Lake main drag in the 1950s.

Rev. Judith Hambleton's work as a traveling interim minister took her throughout Minnesota, where she gathered many stories. She now lives in Tucson, Arizona and visits her family in the Twin Cities area whenever she can find the time.

The Apology
by Richard Hall

As kids with great curiosity, our eyes and ears didn't miss much that took place in our neighborhood. One hot, dry summer day, I was looking for worms and discovered an ash pile on the side of an outhouse. Here I found big fat night crawlers and large white grub worms, and I called it my secret place. It was the one place that I kept secret and didn't tell the other kids in the neighborhood about.

The lady who lived there was one of the more refined women in our part of town. She took great pride in her ability to landscape and decorate. In her battle to camouflage their outhouse, she had her husband put up a large white lattice to shield the door from view. Then she surrounded the building with tall sunflowers and planted all kinds of flowers to help kill the smell. The lattice was covered with honeysuckles, and around the outside of the outhouse were castor beans and rose bushes. The path leading to the outhouse was lined with geraniums. I had been there many times before, and the lady told me I could dig for worms as long as I didn't disturb her flowers.

She was a talking machine, and I was a good listener. I thought we had a pretty good relationship until one day when I told her, "I don't know of anyone with as many pretty flowers, but they don't change the smell of your outhouse, and I don't know of any other outhouse that smells as bad as yours."

Well, I learned right then and there that it doesn't always pay to be honest. She turned all white, and her lips started trembling. Then a crimson flame flushed her cheeks, and she started yelling, "Little boy, I don't appreciate what you just said one bit. I won't allow you to talk that way."

I had seen my father's face turn red when he got mad at me, but I had never seen anyone else get so mad and excited at me before. I was scared to death, and in one quick jump I was on my feet. I was trapped with a fence behind me, and she was on the path in front of me. Then she yelled, "Young man, put those worms back in the ash pile, and don't you ever come back!"

Silently and without any hesitation, even though all my worms didn't belong to her ash pile, I dumped the worms, informing her that the can was mine and I was keeping it. Seeing my chance, I ducked and ran past her. When I was out of her reach, I turned on my heels and yelled that I didn't want her old worms anyway. They stank so bad that the fish wouldn't even eat them. And then I ran as if the devil was chasing me.

Many years later, after I was out of the service, I learned that the woman felt guilty, and she went to my dad and told him the whole story, and she wanted to apologize to me. My father had another idea, however, and he was going to teach me a lesson I wouldn't forget.

My father was old fashioned, and he didn't like me mouthing off to adults. Since this woman's husband was one of my father's gas station customers, this made things even worse. When he came to supper he told me that I was going to have to return to this woman's house and tell her I was sorry. He called it an apology, and I didn't even know what that meant because I had never done it before. I sure didn't know what I was getting myself into.

The next day, my father came home for lunch early and gave me a haircut. Like many others at that time, we didn't have a bathtub or shower, so he brought in the wash tub from the shed and heated a large teakettle of water. I had to take a bath in the middle of the day, which I wasn't used to because I usually took baths before I went to bed. Then he clipped my toenails and fingernails and even had me brush my teeth. What next! All the while, my father was very serious and hardly said a word. Putting me through that whole ordeal, he must have been chuckling to himself. I knew the price I would pay if I grumbled or complained so I didn't say anything.

I had to put on my one white dress shirt, but over the summer I had outgrown my school pants, and I wouldn't be getting a new pair until school started. My feet were like leather from going barefoot all summer, and the only shoes I had were high tops. They were all scuffed, run over at the heels, and they pinched my feet. My dad took a rag and wiped them, but it didn't help much. I plastered my hair down with water.

Most of us kid wore straw hats, and I very seldom went anywhere without mine. They were made of dry hay and had a wide brim that shielded your eyes from the sun. My hat was way too big after my haircut, and the only things that kept it from falling over my face were my ears that stuck out from wearing the straw hat all summer.

I took one last look at my fishing pole, my bed, and house, like I was never going to see them again. I thought about running out the back door, but I didn't know where to go. Without raising my head and almost without breathing, I slowly marched down the street. Every once in awhile I would turn and look back at our house until I couldn't see it anymore. All the while I kept thinking, "Those damn night crawlers. I always had more luck with red worms anyway."

When I reached the woman's house, my knees were weak, and I was suffering from a lack of nerve. Somehow I reached the large front porch, not knowing what to expect. I was able to take a deep breath before rapping at the door. As I peeked through the large oval door window, I could see the woman's outline approaching, and I wanted to run. She opened the door, and for a moment we just gazed at each other without saying anything. There was a glint in her eyes that seemed to be half a twinkle and half a frown, but she looked pleasant, and she was calm.

I took off my hat, like I was supposed to do. My dad had instructed me as to what to say, but when I saw her I got so nervous that I forgot everything and stammered, "I'm sorry your outhouse stinks."

I was about to put my hat back on and take off running when she burst out laughing. There was a sparkle in her eyes as she said she accepted my apology. That broke the ice, and she very nicely invited me into the house. She told me to forget the past and that I could dig worms in her ash pile any time. She showed me around her big house and told me to sit at the large kitchen table. Then she made the mistake of setting a large platter of freshly baked sugar and ginger cookies and a glass of milk in front of me. The story of Hansel and Gretel kept popping up into my mind, but the cookies were so good that it didn't prevent me from eating them all. Just like before, she talked and I listened.

When it was time to go, she brought out a large box of chocolates. I had shared chocolate candy bars before, like Three Musketeers, but never in my life had I seen a large box of chocolates. She let me look them over, and then I chose a piece. I remember how good it was, and I didn't ask for another. Then she picked one out and gave it to me to take home to my little sister.

The sun was hot that day, and being a small boy, I took the long way home. The chocolate was melting, so I kept switching hands and licking the mess that it made. Before long all the chocolate had disappeared.

A few days later, I was going fishing again and needed worms, so I went back to the woman's ash pile. She came out, she started talking like she always did, and we got along just fine. But I did notice that her husband was putting coal oil and some kind of white powder in the outhouse and on the ash pile. It wasn't good for the worms, but after that, the outhouse didn't smell half bad.

Austin native Richard Hall worked at Hormel and wrote several books with original pen and ink drawings. This and the story that follows are from his book "Child of the Great Depression," which is available at the Mower County Historical Society. It was reprinted with permission from Adams historian, Margie Meier.

A Stinky Little Town
by Richard Hall

Some people find odors repugnant, while others seem to take them in stride. Some of my recollections of my old home town involve the smells that to a small boy seemed absolutely putrid.

No one mistook Austin's main industry for a perfume factory. The worst smells came from the very large Hormel packing plant and its adjoining stockyard and pasture. Bordering the plant and flowing through town was the Red Cedar River. It was not a secret that some plant waste material polluted the river, and at times there was a thick, stinking scum on the water. From time to time, just outside the plant, you could see raw sewage being dispensed out of the large drain tiles that emptied from the plant into the river. This fermented decay laid along the shoreline until we were blessed with a heavy rain that would wash the accumulation over the dam.

On the south side of town we had the city disposal plant that did its best to compete with the packing plant for the rankest odor in town, but which usually ranked only second. The railroad yards ranked third. In those days, livestock was shipped in by rail, and the packing plant received 30 to 40 rail cars of livestock a day. There were always cars of livestock and lots of empty, dirty cars standing in the yard. Because animals, lumber, coal, oil, and produce were all shipped by rail, there were many different kinds of smells in the freight yards. While some odors were not particularly offensive, they were smells I will never forget.

The railroad odor had one big advantage over the other two kinds of smells. The coal-fed locomotives with their billowing black smoke that covered the buildings with soot kind of choked out the other smells associated with the yards. The people who worked for the railroad took great pride in the fact that the public liked the unpleasant odor of the yards the best of the three.

As if all this wasn't enough, every block on the outskirts of town had several outdoor toilets. Even the people who had sewer and water kept their old outhouses. I don't know if it was because of the nostalgic memories or if they kept them for emergencies.

As my thoughts tend to wander, it was not my intention to write on this most unusual subject, and I can understand why it has been all but ignored by historians. I can't help but think that the outhouse played a big part in the history, growth and mobility of the people of my time. The outdoor toilet was known by many names, such as outhouse, back house, privy, reading room, library, latrine, outdoor telephone booth, and a few crude names that I was quick to learn as a small boy.

As an admiring youngster, I watched the building of a number of outhouses by our local fathers and carpenters. Many things had to be taken into consideration. Should the building be prominent and a friend to all? Or should you try to hide it from the public? Should it be attached to the wood or coal shed, chicken house or barn? If not, it had better be fastened down well to prevent the boys from having their fun on Halloween. You could save a lot of extra trips if you put it near other buildings. Someone would return to the house with an arm full of wood, a bucket of coal or a basket of eggs.

The distance from the house was an important consideration too. If it was too close, the prevailing wind could be a factor, and you couldn't open your bedroom window on hot nights. It was best if the path was along a fence, a clothesline, or had white painted rocks along the sides for guidance on dark or stormy nights.

Once the spot was chosen, a hole had to be dug. This was governed by how many were going to be using it, how long the family intended to live there, how hard the ground was and who had to dig the hole. You could always tell the shiftless ones because their holes were very shallow, whereas some of the ambitious ones struck water while digging

Outhouses could become pretty dilapidated, and some had to be rebuilt. I always knew in advance when a new one was going to be built or a new hole was going to be dug. The holes were all dug by hand, and if I could get there before they dug too deep, I could find lots of angle worms without doing all the hard work.

As a small boy, even with an untrained eye, I couldn't help but compare outhouses for quality, style and design. There was a great deal of difference in the quality of materials. The decision had to be made whether to use gyp lap, batten tar paper, or siding. I liked the outhouse to be the same design and color as the house. Was the roof to be flat, pitched, hip or shed? Did the door swing in or out? Lack of ventilation made the foul air sickening, so most of the doors swung in so you could control the ventilation with your toe and leave the door open just enough so you could close it quickly if you heard someone coming.

Whistling, singing, humming or stomping your feet was mandatory when you approached the outhouse. You never could tell what might be down in the hole. Once inside and wanting to warn anything that might not have heard you approaching and might still be there, you raised the seat cover and let it slam real hard.

It was very important that the building wasn't sagging, so you could keep the door closed when nobody was using the outhouse. If it was left open, it wasn't unusual to find dogs, cats, or chickens wandering around in there. In most cases, you didn't find the evidence until you had to go out there on a pitch black night.

When it came to outhouses, I always marveled at the many different kinds of decorations that some of them had. Many had old rusty horseshoes nailed above their doors. I was told that a horseshoe above the door brought good luck. I couldn't figure out why you needed good luck going into an outhouse. You could always tell who the sportsmen were because they would nail their deer horns or large fish heads on the side of their outhouses for the public to admire.

Building a new outhouse caused much family debate. The height of the seat was important, and most of them that I remember were too high for little kids. How well I remember how adults would take me out there when I was little and say, "I'll be right outside the door." I had the feeling they were gone forever so I would keep yelling, "Are you still there?"

I remember being so small that I couldn't bend my knees, so I had to go with my legs out straight. I thought I might jack knife through it the hole, so I would straighten my arms on each side to brace myself.

Hole cutting was considered an art because the size and shape of each family member had to be taken into consideration. Did the family prefer round, oval, or heart-shaped holes? Square ones were out of the question. Was there to be one small hole, or were they all to be the same? A small hole was drilled with a brace and bit, and then the large hole cut with a keyhole saw. The edges had to be rasped and sanded, and some were left rough to discourage long visits.

At times when I was small, I thought an outhouse was a delightful place to be. It was an escape from some demanding chores and cooler than being out in the hot sun. On rainy days it was a haven with the sound of rain on the roof. Even if you looked at the Sears or Wards catalog a hundred times the winter before, it seemed like you always found something that you had never seen before when reading it in the outhouse.

In the corner of the outhouse we had an orange crate, divided in the middle, with red corn cobs on one side and white corn cobs on the other for our country relatives. Apples and oranges we bought were wrapped in pink, peach or yellow tissue paper. Each of us kids got to have two tissues, and the rest were saved for when some of our big city relatives came to visit.

It was common for men and boys to carry jack knives, and when they had time they would carve their initials or name on the inside wall or along the seat boards. In some of the older outhouses, you could trace several generations of the same family tree.

Outhouses were a Mecca for rats, mice, spiders, flies, crickets, bees and birds. There was no better place or time to learn about spiders than when sitting in an outhouse. It was fun to watch them in their webs. You would be deep in observation when all of a sudden a big horse fly or mosquito would take a nip out of you and bring you back to reality.

Our town was a breeding ground for flies of all kinds and sizes. I don't think there was a town in the country with more flies per capita. Whenever we got a new fly swatter, the old one found its way to the outhouse. You never had to hang it up because it was always in use. Try as we might, we couldn't catch up with the fly population until we had a good frost. We tried using fly tape inside the outhouse, and I remember one time our tape had turned black with hornets. They had a nest in back of the outhouse under the eaves. Sometimes they got so bad that you couldn't even get into the outhouse and had to make do the best you could until your father got home and made a torch and burned them out. Sparrows would find their way into the outhouse and build their nests on the ledge above the door. They would watch me with their beady black eyes as I sat there, and I wondered what they were thinking.

Those with outhouses didn't have a sewer so several times a day they put table scraps, bath water and dishwater into a bucket and dumped it on the ash pile next to the outhouse or in the garden. This drew rats and mice, and you could see them feeding by the ash pile, where they would dig holes for nests.

Whenever a dog got within a block of the ash pile, he'd go over to explore it. They never missed sprinkling the corner of the outhouse right by the door before they continued on their way. This kind of environment drew all kinds of bugs, flies and gnats so it became a natural feeding place for frogs, toads and snakes.

They say that homing pigeons can find their way home for hundreds of miles. Ants will find their way home from great distances, and you can drop off a cat on the other side of a big city and it will find its way home. Well, we had a kid who could do better than that. I remember one time when I was fishing by Falling Logs with some older kids, and we stayed until after dark. All the lights were out when we passed through Mapleview and the outskirts of Austin. I had no idea where we were in the pitch black. You couldn't see your hand in front of your face, but he always knew where we were. He said his nose told him the way. He couldn't explain it, but said it was just a gift.

We had a number of ethnic groups in town. When the cabbage was ripe, the Germans made sauerkraut. Then came the Irish Mulligan stew. There was also a season for smoked fish and lutefisk. Their odors had no boundaries, and on a hot night when the wind was in the wrong direction you could hear, "Those Germans and their damn sauerkraut," or "I told you they brought in a shipment of lutefisk." When windows started banging down it sounded like a war breaking out.

Spring! Sometimes I shudder at the thought of those first few days with everything exposed and the drying wind coming across the little town. The smell of spring was different because it put you close to nature. Many homes were cold with no basement or just a cellar so people would nail tar paper or a pink building paper around their foundation and nail laths to hold the paper in place.

In the fall they would have a farmer bring in a load or two of manure. If your order went in early, you got horse or cow manure, but after that you had to take what you could get. They would pack it around the foundation of their house for insulation. If you were fortunate enough to get snow or a good frost, you didn't notice the smell so much, but with the first warm days of spring, things changed. The juices started to run, and their vapors filled the air.

The farmer would come back in spring with his team to plow the garden. Just for good measure, he might bring another load of manure. We didn't have garbage haulers like we do today so the farmer would plow the ashes under when he plowed the garden, pick up the trash and put it in gunny sacks, and dump it in some gully on his farm.

About this same time, we would get a spring rain, and with the spring hog run at Hormel, the air would be so thick you could cut it with a knife. The town natives were able to endure the unpleasant odor, but you could always tell a bewildered stranger who would be holding his nose or coughing. His eyes would be watering, and his face would be chalk white. You could hear him gasp, "What is that smell?" The towns- people would just smile and say, "You should have been here last week," or "That's George hanging his feet out the window."

As I turn on the water or flush the toilet today, I have no desire to return to those good old days. My mind goes back, and I remember the wind blowing through the cracks in the outhouse on a dark night. I re- member that at bedtime during winter, you had to put on your coat and overshoes. Someone would light the lantern or grab the kerosene lamp, and you thought it was going to be a quick trip. But everyone had to come along, even the dog and cat, and you would stand shivering, waiting your turn. I don't need a horseshoe over my bathroom door to remind me know how lucky I am.

When a Dime Could Take You Somewhere
by Marian Westrum

I was born on a farm near Randolph in Dakota County. When I was little, we visited Grandma and Grandpa near Clarks Grove in Freeborn County a couple of times each year. When I was 7, I stayed a week with them, and I didn't get homesick because Aunt Stella and Uncle Bob were still living at home.

Uncle Bob was my mother's youngest brother, and because he was only five years older than me, he was more like an older brother. I slept with Stella, who was eleven years older than me, in her three-quarter sized bed. I wonder now if she got tired of me, but I can't ask her because she is gone. What I do know is that she was always happy to see me.

In 1931, when I was 10, we left the farm because of the Great Depression and moved to Albert Lea. My dad hoped he would be able to find work at the Wilson Packing Plant, and he did. The move meant that I would be able to visit Grandma and Grandpa more often.

When I was 12, I began the ritual of walking from our home on Pleasant Avenue to the Jefferson Bus Depot in the Hotel Albert in downtown Albert Lea. Several times each summer I would buy a ticket for 10 cents and ride the bus out to the corner where the Clarks Grove Golf Course is now located. After getting off the bus, I would walk a half mile to the farm of my grandparents, Andrew C. and Maren Christiansen Jensen.

I loved Grandma and Grandpa Jensen very much. They were my mother's parents who had emigrated from Denmark in 1892 before they were married. Because they were not married, they could both get jobs when they arrived. They married in 1894 and had nine children, including two sets of twins.

In their living room was a painting of Grandpa as a young man, and he was really handsome. All the years I knew my grandma, she had white hair fixed in a roll at the top of her head, and Grandpa had very little hair left.

Their farm was just a couple of miles from Clarks Grove. A big sign at the driveway read, "Willow Dale Dairy Farm." I do not know if Grandma and Grandpa named the farm or the sign was there when they bought it.

South of the house was a pond with willow trees around half of it, and willow trees stood at other places on the farm. I do not remember whether the trees died or they were cut down when the pond was drained to make more room for crops.

Grandpa had a large dairy herd of registered Holsteins. All the cows had names on their stalls, and Grandpa always claimed they responded to their names. He had horses too, since he had no tractor. But he did have a Model T Ford.

I had two younger brothers, Ray and Forry. Ray liked to stay at Grandma and Grandpa's sometimes, but Forry always said he didn't like country air. My brother Ray remembers that Grandpa had five horses. He had a Belgian named Duke and a team of two smaller horses. He had two white horses that Uncle Tony, his oldest son, had given him when he quit farming to start his trucking business.

On one visit, I arrived just as they were eating breakfast. Grandpa was always a bit perturbed that I wanted my egg fried hard. That morning he asked if I would do something for him, and I said I would. "Have Grandma fry your egg medium, and see if you like it that way." I did, and I eat my eggs that way to this day.

I liked visiting because Grandma would let me help her gather eggs in the henhouse, set the table, and best of all, make cookies. It was also my job to go fetch the mail so I would watch to see when the mailman came. He always had to stop because the daily paper came in the mail.

My grandparents were great believers in naps, probably because they got up so early to milk the cows. On their screened-in porch they had a couch. After lunch I had to rest there, and more often than not I fell asleep. Grandma dozed in her rocker, Stella went to her room, and Grandpa and Bob slept right out on the lawn.

I loved those visits to my grandparents' farm, but after I got to be a teenager, I was expected to earn a little money so I did housework for other people for 15 cents an hour, and I had to help my folks take care of my younger siblings. I didn't have so much time to take those trips out to Clarks Grove.

My grandparents retired and moved to town, and Bob took over the farm. They died in the early '50s. Stella got married and moved to Decorah, Iowa, but Bob continued to live on the family farm until he died in 1985. My two kids visited the farm quite often, and we had many family reunions there. We always drove them from Albert Lea to Clarks Grove, however. They never got to ride the bus for a dime.

Grandma Maren Christianson, Stella, Marian and Dexter, 1945

Albert Lea resident Marian Porter Westrum has a son, a daughter, two grandchildren, and two step grandchildren. She won acclaim as a golfer for many years, and now enjoys writing.

Pa
by Bill King

My brother and I would call him Pa. My sisters, more cultured and sophisticated, called him Dad or Father.

His name was Frank King, and he lived all of his life in Freeborn County. From the moment he was born the cards were stacked against him. His mother died in childbirth, his father left within a couple of days, his brothers and sisters were sent to live with different relatives, and he went to spend his growing up years at Grandma's house. Grandma's house is cool if it's just once in awhile, but living there full time became complicated as uncles became brothers and aunts became sisters and cousins became nephews and nieces.

He led an average life, like any kid on a farm. The rest of the family were all older, and his nephews and nieces were his age or older. He didn't even get to keep his own name; his birth name was George Franklin, but there already was a George, so he became Franklin George. Growing up on the farm during the Depession meant you had a lot of potatoes and eggs to eat, but you were responsible for helping to provide the food, and you went about making your own fun.

After finishing the required eighth grade, he eventually went to Austin Vocational School and left with a certificate in auto mechanics. His skills as an auto mechanic went unused during World War II, but his job as a driver and welder for Izzy Waterman were considered essential to the war effort. He never left town.

Raising a family and working for Izzy kept us on Charles Street. This was not something to brag about, but it provided his family with the knowledge that the only way out was up.

Pa always hunted with a single shot rifle or a long tom shot gun. One shot, one bird or squirrel for the pot.

I worked at Wilson's Packing House for a few years, and at lunch, the hunters would brag about their hunting skills over the previous weekend. Because of my lack of hunting skills and lack of interest, I started telling the guys stories of my dad and his skill with guns. I told about Dad shooting coins at 60 feet or shooting pigeons on the fly from the hay mow doors with a .22 rifle. After the look of astonishment, they laughed and said it couldn't be done.

The Wilson workers commented that if he was that good, he should be shooting for some company and traveling to shooting matches showing off his skills.

Over time I forgot about it until a couple of months ago. A cousin of mine commented on how he and his family would show up at our house on Charles Street and how my Dad would go outside and start to shoot. This was not a bad thing at the very end of Charles Street. The neighbors would just say, "Frank's at it again." Everyone would laugh and wonder if he would ever miss a shot.

Pa had his duties. He had a family to support, and hunting put food on the table. Shooting for fun and winning prizes was for other people. Shells cost money, and money bought food and paid bills. You make choices, and you live with them.

Frank's family included an attractive, strong wife, two daughters who became secretaries, a daughter with a bachelor's degree in medical records, a son who retired as an Army major and earned a master's degree in procurement, and a self-employed barber. Not bad for an orphan.

Frank King

Albert Lea resident Bill King is a barber who enjoys history.

Breaking a Wild Lawn Mower
by Betty Jean Rueckert Collins

The temperature had dropped to 70 after last week's hot and humid spell, and it seemed like a good day to mow the lawn. It was Saturday morning, and Tom was eager to try out his new toy, a zero radius turning Schweiss mower.

The May tornado that hit our farm had ruined a lot of things, including our lawn mower. The not-so-old Snapper zero-radius model Z2000 literally flew apart when Tom, my husband, was mowing some knee-high grass around the grain bins. After one swath around the bins, the belts broke, sending the entire electrical system on a flight to somewhere.

Tom and Bob, the hired hand, investigated their dilemma while I left to run errands. While I was gone they drove to the dealership where the mower had been purchased. When I returned I saw two men standing over the mower. Bob held his cap and scratched his head while Tom towered over the mower holding some papers, still puzzled by the circumstances of its breakdown. I figured something was up when I saw their half-parted smiles say, "Don't ask."

"I traded mowers," Tom said as he handed me the brochure. My eyes quickly vacillated between his and Bob's expressions as I caught Bob glancing between Tom and me. I already knew I didn't want to hear what they had bought. "Be about ten days before we get it," Tom added.

Looking at the brochure, I thought the mower seemed monstrous, photographed from a low vantage point. Pictures can be deceiving, right? Wrong!

"You'll be able to get your mowing done and cover a lot more ground faster with this one," he told me. "It has a 72 inch deck."

"Seventy-two inches!" I gasped. "My god, I can hardly squeeze sixty inches into some places. How am I ever going to get twelve more inches in and around those trees?"

All Tom said was, "Don't get upset until you try it." What is this mentality that farming men have that never lets the wife have a say in the purchase of a machine she is expected to operate?

The following week the new lawn mower arrived. Tom was given a brief set of instructions and little else for orientation. He drove the mower to the shed, where it sat for another week.

The second time Tom drove it, showing off for some out-of-state company, the mower bounced and leaped as it moved along the circle drive. I had never seen a mower buck like a horse, but this one did just that during the brief demonstration.

Soon after, I worked at my sewing machine in the kitchen while Tom went out to mow. In a few minutes I heard him and the mower coming up the lawn toward the house. I met him at the back door and emphatically urged him to go someplace else first because we already knew the mower acted like a wild bronco. More accurately, I hollered and pointed to the center yard. "You got 40 acres of yard right out in the middle. Go out THERE and practice." It was like talking to the deaf.

I really didn't want that big thing so close to my few remaining flowers that had survived the horrors of weather. Besides, that monster machine simply wouldn't fit near the house.

In the meantime, I thought, "I'll fix you." I quickly went to the shed for the small old Snapper to mow around the house myself. Anything to keep him away from the house. Much to my disappointment, it had a flat tire. Mad and disgusted, I stomped back to the house with no choice but to go back to my sewing machine and hope for the best.

Sure enough, Tom soon rode around the front of the house, heading straight for my flower bed, the tightest corner of the yard. He sat in the saddle, hanging on to the T bar saddle horn with his left hand and tightly gripping the adjacent joy stick with his right. He looked like a bronco rider, with the mower leaping and lunging, trying to throw the determined rider.

The seconds were counting as destruction unfolded. In a flash, I flew out the back door waving my arms wildly as I charged around the corner of the house yelling and cursing, "Stop it. Get that damn thing out of here and away from my flowers. I told you to stay away from the house! Get the hell out of here!"

I could hear his deep voice bellowing above the roar of the mower as he hollered back, "Get out of the way! Damn it, Get out of the way." The moss roses were being smashed from the back bucking rear wheels, and the scarlet runner climbing bean and other newly-planted perennials were next in line for attack. The joystick vibrated wildly as the mower lunged forward into the bird feeder and pole. The feeder flew one way, and the pole bent down, submitting to its second assault this season.

Tom finally tamed the jolting machine, and we both shouted angry words. I was yelling because he had gotten himself into the tight spot I had warned him about, and he was shouting because he feared I might get hurt by the charging mower. After catching his breath, he high-tailed it back to the dealership. In defense of their machine, they tried to give pointers and reassurance that it takes time to get the feel of the fast joy-stick action. He needed to go easy on the touch and a bit slower on the throttle. A mechanic said the first time he drove one he nearly wiped out the shop before getting his runaway mower under control.

Tom came home, not exactly satisfied with the results of his trip to the dealer, but he got back on the mower to try again. This time, still near the house, he started on the other side outlining around the big evergreen trees. One half round later, I heard the engine quit and saw Tom walk past the kitchen window toward the back door. He set something down and headed back past the kitchen window. As he passed the window I hollered, "Now what's the matter?"

With his head down and with a sheepish look on his face, he said, "A wheel fell off, and I ran over it with the blades." My eyes opened like silver dollars. Sure enough, one of the little front wheels looked like mince-meat. Tom called the dealership. An employee answered the phone but told him they were closed until Monday morning. Tom slumped in his chair defeated and said, "I got a big lump in my stomach. That machine cost me $6000, and I think it's a lemon."

He ate a big dinner but suffered major heartburn the rest of that afternoon and evening. We thought out loud to each other about the high probability that we wouldn't get all the lawn mowed this year. The tattered pattern of lawn evidenced an unfinished job. For the time being though, the flowers were safe.

Tom's theory was that the hydraulics could be responsible for the machine's jump-like-a-jackrabbit disposition, which jiggled the joystick out of control. The dealer thought it was just Tom's technique, and the manufacturer thought it could be a loose cable. The mechanic would not be out until Tuesday afternoon with the part Tom ordered and to observe Tom's driving skills. Tom said, "He can drive it and see for himself."

Early Monday morning Tom dropped off the shredded wheel at the dealer, and late Tuesday afternoon the mechanic arrived with a new wheel. Some of the pieces necessary for the fix had flown off with the wheel so Tom and I took our two heavy-duty magnets to comb the lawn. We found enough pieces to make it work.

With the mower all back together again, the mechanic saddled up and smoothly drove off with no bucking, no kicking, and no jumping. "It's all in the touch," he said with a smile.

"Just like a sensitive, well-trained, neck-reining horse, right?"

"I'm a rider too," he replied. "You're right. Here you take it."

I climbed on from the left, just like mounting my horse Safieh, and off I went to circle the center ring, neck reined her through the four maple trees, reined in for a one-eighty, and back to the finish line. Riding that mower was just like handling my barrel and pole racing horse while sitting on one of my Shetland ponies, much closer to the ground. Just for the heck of it, I kicked her in gear for the buck, and then reined her in for control. NO problem. It was all a matter of touch. The mechanic wished us good luck, and I went on to tackle a much-neglected lawn.

Betty Jean Collins is a retired nurse, and her husband is a retired farmer. They live in Minnesota Lake and winter in Arizona. They have two adult daughters.

Athena Rose and Her Dime
by Anastasia "Stacy" Vellas

Walter Cummings and his wife Marian started coming to our place near Swatara in 1938. Daddy had written to Montgomery Ward in St. Paul offering to ship strawberry plants for them if they had orders to fill in the spring. They sent Walter Cummings to our house to make arrangements. Walter and Daddy made a deal, and they shook hands.

When spring arrived, we began shipping strawberry plants to people all over the state and to nearby states. That was the most money Daddy had made in many, many years. Daddy, Connie, Rose and I would dig up runners that grew out from the big strawberry plants, separate their roots, and tie them in bundles of 12. Daddy would count out each order, pack some damp dirt around the roots, wrap them in butcher paper, put them in a box, and ship them directly to the people who ordered them.

Every two or three days he took plants to the Swatara post office. Earl Heath would take care of them there, bag them and ship by train. Daddy shipped young strawberry plants from April, as soon as the plants started putting off runners (new plants) until past the middle of May.

Walter and Marian Cummings liked the Vellas family and often came to visit in the fall. Dad invited Walter to go duck hunting with him. Later he invited Walter to go deer hunting, and there was always a deer for Walter to take home to St. Paul. Walter would tie the deer on his fender to show off his skill on his way home. Each fall Walter and Marian would stay a few days during hunting season, sleep at our house, and eat with us. Mama cooked a lot of food then, and we had plenty. They both smoked so Mama decided she would smoke too. But she soon got tired of that and quit. I doubt that she ever inhaled. It was just a big city idea that she tried for awhile.

At Christmas the Cummings sent us two big boxes of clothes and things they had gathered from relatives in St. Paul for our family. Some clothes could be made into dresses for Mama and us girls. Sometimes there were coats. It was such fun to go through those boxes. Mama could sew so she was grateful to get hand-me-downs. Marian and Walter bought something for each one of us kids. They sent my sister Rose a pretty doll, and they sent me a mirror and hairbrush set because I was older. I was about 12, but I would really have liked a doll too. I never had a nice doll. They sent Connie a small tractor.

My sister Rose was a backwoods kid, and she would not talk to Marian and Walter. As soon as Rose saw them come in the door, she would run and hide under the bed. Walter would try to coax her to come out. He would offer her candy or money or something he thought she would like, but still she would not come out. He tried to get her to talk, but she wouldn't talk to him. Finally, after many months, he spoke to her, and she answered him. Walter gave her a dime, a whole dime.

Oh, how she cherished that dime. She took one of Daddy's big square handkerchiefs and carefully rolled her dime up in a corner and then tied the handkerchief around the dime in a knot. She carried that dime everywhere she went. She carried it around the farm. She took it to school with her. She even took it to bed with her. She would hold it up for us to see, and then she would smirk. She'd dangle it and smile at us. She loved to taunt and tease. Oh, how we wanted to hurt her.

That fall, Marian Cummings took pictures of the Vellas family with her husband Walter, and there was Rose with a handkerchief dangling from her hand.

A couple of months later, Rose decided she would spend a penny of her dime for candy. She would walk around in front of us waving her handkerchief and gloat, "I'm going to buy a penny candy at Trepanier's store!" She made a big show of the procedure. She held the handkerchief up and waved it around in the air to taunt us. Then she slowly undid the knot in the handkerchief, looking up to be sure we were watching. When the knot finally came apart, she just stood there agape---there was a STICK! Instead of a dime in her handkerchief, all this time she had been carrying around a stick. She looked at that stick, and she turned pale. She started crying, turned and ran away and hid. Her wonderful dime was gone. She had been gloating and carrying a stick around in her handkerchief.

Connie finally owned up to taking the dime out of the handkerchief and replacing it with a stick that he had carved into the shape of a dime. Daddy didn't punish him; he just said, "You are a bad boy doin' that to your sister."

Connie didn't replace the money. There was no money. We might go to town four or five times a year. Sometimes Daddy would tell us we could pick out a penny candy at the store. But even if Connie gave up his penny, it would take at least two years to give Rose back her dime. Rose never forgot her first dime. She would tell the story about her lost dime over and over throughout the years.

Rose, on the right, proudly clutches her dime wrapped in a handkerchief as we pose for Mrs. Cummings at our house in Swatara

Stacy Vellas and her family moved from Swatara in northern Minnesota to California in 1944. She worked as a waitress and a field worker, and in 1973 she became a teacher. The mother of five wonderful sons, she lives near Brawley, California and loves to write.

The Summer of 1941 and the Big Heist
by Anastasia "Stacy" Vellas

I can tell this story now. The statute of limitations is past, and we can't be arrested, or so my brother Connie said.

Breakfast was over. I could hear Mama in the kitchen rattling pans as she finished washing dishes. I wriggled into one of last fall's flowered cotton dresses. Connie put on a pair of faded overalls with legs that were several inches too short. Oh well, no one lived close enough to see how we dressed.

Oh, dear! Mama in the kitchen began yelling. She had fits of anger about one thing or another. I hurried out the door and down the steps of the old green school house, where we were living in 1941, the year after the twins were born. If Mama noticed me, she would start in on me about one of my many infractions. "Come on, Connie, let's get out of here!" I urged.

Over the winter we had outgrown the shoes Mama had bought in the fall, so we walked to the main road barefooted. We crossed the yard overgrown with grass grown thick and tall from many summer rains. We hurried along until we were far enough away to be out of hearing range in case Mama called.

"What shall we to do today?" Connie asked.

"I don't know. Shall we take the back road to the old Hansen place at Lake Edna?" I suggested. The Hansen family had moved and built a new house on McKinney Lake.

Across the road from our place was an old wagon road from the time of homesteaders and loggers, overgrown but still visible. "Let's take the wagon road. It will come out on White Elk Road, I think."

"Okay," said Connie.

We crossed the main road in our bare feet. The old tote road dipped down from the main road and followed the hill above the swamp, overgrown with bushes and tall ferns. We cut trail as we went, stepping around bushes and over trees that had fallen. About a mile farther on we came out onto White Elk Road. The WPA had cleared trees on each side, and the deep ruts were wide enough for a car or pickup to drive into the back country. This was one of many roads that hadn't been used since the days of teams and wagons that brought my grandfather to the north woods to take out a homestead.

A snort startled us. From the side of the road a deer entered the clearing. Seeing us standing there, the deer in one jump cleared the road. With two more high jumps and a flash of its white tail, it disappeared into the woods. "Did you see that?" I asked with surprise, "It jumped clear across the road and kicked up his heels at us."

There were chokecherry bushes along the road. The chokecherries were ripe so we ate our fill and kept walking. The cherries puckered my mouth, but they were good and filling, and we might not be home for dinner.

The summer sun was warm as we continued on down the road. A meadowlark sang in the tall grass as a flock of Canadian geese flew high in the clear blue sky on their way to Otter Lake. About half a mile down the road, a smaller dirt road turned off to the left. What could be down this road? We turned in and discovered a gate with a cable stretched across the road.

"Let's see what's down this road," I said. Connie willingly followed my lead. There was no fence on either side of the gate so we went around the posts and followed the road. It was green everywhere--green grass, green bushes and poplar trees with their whispering green leaves. The trees along the side of the road reached out their branches making a cool, shading arch over the road. In a short time we came out into a clearing.

On the left as we entered the clearing we spied a boathouse with a wire fence around it. On the south side it had a gate with a heavy padlock. On the right, secluded among pine trees, we could see a small summer cottage owned by city people who only came out a few times a year. Beyond the house, the yard sloped down to a boat landing on Otter Lake.

"Do you think anyone is here?" I whispered to Connie. "I don't hear anything." We listened intently, ready to move back quietly into the brush at the slightest sound.

"I don't see a car. Let's go see what's here," Connie whispered. We waited a few more minutes and scouted the area. No one was there. We talked in hushed voices, fearing someone would come up the road behind and find us on their place.

Cautiously we approached the boathouse. "Look Connie, two boats--and they look new," I whispered.

He remarked, "I'd sure like to have that one if we could get it to our boat landing on Moose River."

Walking over to the small tool shed, I pushed on the door. The hinges were loose, and the latch came free as the door opened. We looked over the shed's contents of shovels, hoes, saws and axes. On one side was, wonder of all wonders, a lawn mower! A green push lawn mower! What a wonderful stroke of luck!

"Look, Connie, we could cut the grass in front of the green school house and have a lawn like the people in town." I said excitedly.

"Well, you can do that if you want, but I'm not going to mow that lawn. It's too big. But I can oil the mower and get it ready for you," he replied.

As we checked out the premises, a chipmunk scurried in front of us. Startled, I jumped back and tried to pretend it didn't scare me. We were a half-mile from the White Elk Road now, and there was not a soul around.

Skulking through knee-deep grass, we again approached the house. The door was locked, and it wouldn't give no matter how much we pushed and pried. Every window was locked solid.

Giving up, we went back to the tool shed. After looking the tools over, Connie chose a sturdy axe, and we returned to the house. "Be careful," I said, "Let me do it. We don't want to damage the door any more than we have to." Taking the axe from him, I split the door's lower panel into three pieces, with one piece leaving jagged edges facing toward the inside.

We carefully removed the panel and crawled through the small hole into a nicely furnished cabin. Walking around through the house, we found nothing interesting. We left the house as we found it and replaced the pieces of the door's panel to keep out the rain.

This is the cabin we broke into. They have added a room on the side.

We returned to the boathouse and hammered on the padlock with the flat side of the axe until it sprang apart. We chose the best boat that was placed on a high frame about three feet off the ground. Lifting it up, over and off the boat stand, we pulled it outside onto the soft grass under the pines.

I picked out two good oars and put them in the boat. Then we closed the gate and put the broken lock back on the hook. Connie took one side of the boat, and I took the other as we pulled it with both hands slowly through the grass down to the sandy shore of the lake.

Silently we slid it into Otter Lake with hardly a splash. We stopped and listened. Had anyone heard the noise? Nothing moved.

While Connie checked the boat for leaks, I went back to the tool shed and hung the axe back on the wall. I looked at the lawn mower again. How I wanted that lawn mower! People in town mowed their lawns, and they had such pretty yards. I had to have it. I reached for the handle and pulled it outside. When I turned it over, I found it didn't make much noise so I pushed it down to the boat. The gentle click, click of the rollers was music to my ears. Connie and I picked it up and lowered it into the boat. I got in, and Connie pushed the boat off from shore. Putting the oars into the oarlocks, I started rowing across the lake toward the old Gressen place and home.

It was getting on into late afternoon as we crossed the lake, pulled up to Gressen's landing, and tossed the anchor onto the sandy beach. Everything was quiet, with only the lonesome cry of a loon echoing across the lake as evening approached.

We lifted the lawn mower out of the boat and set it on the ground. I turned it over, and we started walking to our green school house taking turns pushing it. As we turned into the yard, we could hear Mama still banging pans and hollering in the kitchen.

"I think we're in time for supper," I said. We hid the mower behind the house and went inside to eat. Bed sure looked good after such a hard day. Being in the middle of a heist didn't mean we were going to lose any sleep. We would deal with the boat tomorrow.

In the morning we got up early. "Connie, we have to get the boat to our landing before somebody finds it and takes it away," I reminded him. As soon as we ate breakfast and finished our chores, we headed for Gressen's landing.

It began as a bright sunny Minnesota day with not a cloud in the sky as we started out on our trek. We dragged the boat onto shore, and with Connie on one side and me on the other, we pulled it along on the grass toward the county road. We passed Gressen's empty house with its sunken roof as we progressed over the hill and down through the open field to the county road. We hid the boat in the tall grass near the main road, and I ran to the top of the hill to see if any cars were coming.

While I watched for cars, Connie pulled the boat across the gravel road into the tall grass on Charley Dixon's old road. We had never been down this road before, but we knew it went past the old Dixon place. We decided that if a car came while we were on Dixon's road, we would lie down in the tall grass next to the boat so they couldn't see us and hope the grass was tall enough so they couldn't see the boat.

The boat was big and heavy for two kids. Every few minutes we would have to stop, drop the boat and rest. When we heard a car, we would drop the boat and lie down to wait for it to go by. After awhile, as we got farther down the road, we couldn't hear cars anymore.

Heading due north about a mile down the old road we came to a clearing. The air was cool, but it was still bright and sunny. Birds sang in the trees as we pulled the boat along. We were excited about our new boat but still very apprehensive about our heist.

After we passed the vacant and decaying Dixon house, the road abruptly ended. What should we do now? Hoping we could reach Moose River, we kept going north straight into the woods. We had no idea how far it would be to the river. After pulling the boat a short distance into the woods past the house, we suddenly came to Moose River, which was much closer than we expected. "Wonderful! Wonderful! We're half-way home, Connie," I said.

We pulled and wrestled with the boat until we got it down the bank and into the river. Then we had another problem. Moose River was only about a foot and a half deep at this time of year. Standing in the water next to the boat, I looked down and saw a crayfish near my foot. I quickly jumped into the boat. We would have to push or pull the boat up river, and I was NOT going to wade in that river with crayfish on the bottom.

So who do you think had to get out and pull that boat up river? That's right; Connie took the rope and began pulling the boat with me in it. I sat there like a queen on her throne. Well, for a while at least.

The river was very narrow, and trees had fallen across it in many places. When we couldn't push limbs aside or lift a tree to go under it, I would have to get out, help pull the boat out of the river around the tree and back into the water, where Connie could take over again pulling upstream. We had gone about a mile up river, over and around fallen trees with my erstwhile brother pulling the boat, before the river suddenly widened and got deep enough so we could row the boat.

All of a sudden, a big black thundercloud came up out of nowhere, and in a few minutes the sun disappeared. It began to thunder and lightning, and rain began coming down in sheets. I rowed the boat as fast as I could, but we were still a long way from our boat landing.

"Let's pull the boat out onto the meadow where Daddy cuts hay," I told Connie. When we reached the meadow, we found the river much wider and deeper. We pulled the boat out of the water and turned it over.

"Let's get under the boat where we'll be safe," I said. We crawled under the boat, but the grass was already wet from rain, and our clothes were soaked. I couldn't stand being under the boat. We were scared to leave and scared to stay. Finally I said, "Connie, we have to make a run for it and get to our old house on the farm. It will be dry there."

Leaving the boat bottom-up, we took off running. We made it to the Harrington Dam and crossed the river. We ran up the old wagon road and past the open fields as rain came down in torrents and the storm raged around us. We were two scared kids. It didn't take us long to reach the tarpaper house on our old homestead and find shelter under its roof.

We stayed about an hour. When the rain stopped, we ran all the way to our green school house. By the time we reached home, our clothes were dry. No one noticed we had been soaking wet as we went on into the house. "Where have you kids been?"

"Oh, just down the road and out in the woods," we told her. She was satisfied with that answer.

The next day was clear and sunny. We walked back, turned over the boat, and put it back into the water. The water was deeper from there to the landing, and the river was clear of trees. I jumped in and rowed the boat up river, around the bay and on to our boat landing on Moose River. We pulled it half way out of the water and dropped anchor. We breathed a sigh of relief when it was done. We were finished, and we were exhausted.

We took the boat out several times after that. Daddy even took it fishing and never asked where it came from. "Somebody left a boat at our landing," he remarked, "I guess we can use it."

The grass was nearly a foot high when I began mowing the lawn at our green school house. I worked so hard to cut it the first time that I had huge blisters on my hands. But in no time our lawn was trim and neat. I kept the lawn mowed at the green school house the rest of the summer. I was so proud of my lawn. No one ever questioned us about where the lawn mower came from.

That fall we moved into town, and the snow came and covered my lawn. No one ever knew until now that I stole a lawn mower and a boat except my brother and now you. And YOU better not tell!

I never considered the possibility that the sheriff might have come right to my door asking where I had gotten the lawn mower. Mama and Daddy never asked where it came from. They should have.

We used the boat until we moved to town. We left all our boats at the Moose River Landing when we left for California. We went back to Minnesota in 1947, and you know what? Some low-life had stolen all our boats!

My Memories of Minnesota
by Anastasia "Stacy" Vellas

*Oh, to see Third Guide again
With its waters running high
And willow branches bending low
When the wind goes whistling by.*

*Across the lake on an evening breeze
Comes the plaintive call of a loon.
It's time that I'm returning home
Though not a bit too soon.*

*To see Moose River crest its bank
As water goes roaring by
Oh, just to be a child again
'Neath that Minnesota sky!*

*With woodland trails to follow each day
And a brother who loved to roam
And parents who let us find our way
As long as we both came home.*

*I had no boundaries to hold me in
Or inhibit my restless soul.
I could wander as far as the day is long
With a line and a fishing pole.*

*With miles of back country to explore
As each season drifted by,
Oh, never was there a child before
Born more lucky than I!*

*Yes, I was rich, much richer then
When I rode old Blackie to plow
Or rowed a boat across Third Guide Lake
Yes, I was much richer than now.*

About Minnesota Memories 5

I have always considered myself a Minnesotan. While living in other states, I enjoyed getting together with fellow Minnesotans to share stories about life in the North Star State. These stories not only entertained, but they refreshed and restored whatever it was about my mind and soul that needed refreshment and restoration.

Five years ago I was teaching in Maryland, and across the hall was another native Minnesotan, Kathy Megyeri. One day, after Kathy sold a story to the *Chicken Soup* publishers, I said, "Somebody should compile a book of stories about life in Minnesota. Every Minnesotan has at least one good true story or recollection, and a compilation of all those stories would make a terrific book." We pitched that idea to publishers, and they pitched it right back.

After recovering from this rejection, we decided that we would take it upon ourselves to compile and publish a book of extraordinary stories by ordinary Minnesota folks. When we contacted old friends, only a few responded and sent stories because many doubted that we would actually publish a book. Undaunted, we confounded those skeptics, wrote some of our own stories, combined them with a few we received from other people, and published *Minnesota Memories* in 2001.

I traveled more than 10,000 miles that first summer, from Grand Marais to Austin and from Adrian to Winona--talking to newspaper reporters and radio interviewers about my *Minnesota Memories* mission. I spoke at county fairs, schools, class reunions, book stores, trade shows, service clubs, church groups and historical societies, inviting ordinary people to send their extraordinary stories for *Minnesota Memories 2*.

Since that time, I have traveled thousands of additional miles meeting people all over Minnesota, collecting and publishing hundreds of their stories in five volumes. This is so much fun that I intend to keep publishing *Minnesota Memories* books until all the great Minnesota stories have been preserved in print--or until I conk out, whichever comes first.

Joan Claire Graham,   Purveyor of Memories

Minnesota Memories 5 features stories
from these towns.

*Two Harbors

*Swatara
*Aiken

*Brainerd
*Milaca
*Foreston
*Minneapolis *St Paul
*Clinton   *M'tonka
              Mills   *Apple
           *Bloomington Valley *Rosemount
        *Morgan   *Northfield
   *Redwood Falls,   *Dundas
                     *Kellogg
        *Mankato   *Owatonna
   *Sveadahl   *St Clair *Waseca   *Winona
  *Kenneth   *MN. Lake
              *Clarks Grove *Hollandale
*Luverne   *Jackson   *Alden *Albert Lea *Austin
           *Frost *Conger   *Hayward

Did you find a story from your town in this book? Do you have a favorite
true story you'd like to share with the world in *Minnesota Memories 6*?
Send stories (and photos) to Minnesota Memories, 439 Lakeview Blvd,
Albert Lea, MN 56007, or email them to MinnMemory@aol.com. To book
a *Minnesota Memories* program at your library, historical society, organization, store or school, use the addresses above or call 507-377-1255.

**Back page special! If you made it all the way to the last paragraph of
the last page, you deserve a break. Order any book from the Minnesota Memories series for $12. For a complete 5-book set, send $57
(check to Minnesota Memories or cash). Postage & tax are included.
What a deal!**